SN

Self-Torture
and
Strenuous Exercise

Self Torture
and
Strenuous Exercise

SELECTED PLAYS

Harry Kondoleon

THEATRE COMMUNICATIONS GROUP 1991

Self Torture and Strenuous Exercise: Selected Plays is published by Theatre Communications Group, Inc., 355 Lexington Ave., New York, NY 10017.

TCG gratefully acknowledges public funds from the National Endowment for the Arts, the New York State Council on the Arts and the New York City Department of Cultural Affairs in addition to the generous support of the following foundations and corporations: Alcoa Foundation; Ameritech Foundation; ARCO Foundation; AT&T Foundation; Citibank; Consolidated Edison Company of New York; Nathan Cummings Foundation; Dayton Hudson Foundation; Exxon Corporation; Ford Foundation; James Irvine Foundation; Jerome Foundation; Andrew W. Mellon Foundation; Metropolitan Life Foundation; National Broadcasting Company; Pew Charitable Trusts; Philip Morris Companies; Scherman Foundation; Shubert Foundation.

The author gratefully acknowledges the contributions of Stephen Soba and Betty Osborn.

Cover photo by Sebastian Li.

Lyrics to "I Put a Spell on You" by Screamin' Jay Hawkins copyright © 1956 Unart Music Corporation. Rights assigned to EMI Catalogue Partnership. All rights controlled and administered by EMI Unart Catalog, Inc. Reprinted by permission.

Kondoleon, Harry.
  Self torture and strenuous exercise: selected plays / Harry Kondoleon.
  Contents: Self torture and strenuous exercise—Christmas on Mars—The vampires—Slacks and tops—Anteroom.
  ISBN 1-55936-037-2 (cloth)—ISBN 1-55936-036-4 (paper)
  I. Title.
  PS3561.0456S44   1991
  812'.54—dc20   91-22125
                                              CIP

Book design and composition by The Sarabande Press

First Edition, October 1991

CONTENTS

To my parents

Self Torture
and
Strenuous Exercise

CHARACTERS

Alvin
Bethany
Carl
Adel

TIME

Fall. Late.

SETTING

The dining room of Alvin and Bethany. There is a round table with
a white tablecloth and the remnants of a late-night supper. There
are dirty plates, half-filled glasses, unfolded napkins, unlit candles
and a centerpiece of flowers. As much occurs on the floor, a raked
stage would be an asset.

Carl, Alvin and Bethany are seated at the table.

Carl: Alvin, I'm in love with another woman.

Alvin: Good! Good for you Carl. I'm glad. When Adel died, I can't
tell you the psychic exhaustion I suffered worrying who you'd
find to take her place. I didn't want to cook. Tell him, Beth. I
just stood at my cutting board, surrounded by raw vegetables,
and thought, why go on? I wanted a sign from above. I wanted
God to say, "Al, go on." Death is so depleting. I know you
loved Adel, but did you know I did? I loved her. I don't mean
I was sleeping with her—I loved her as a spiritual sister, are
you following me? Then I thought how everything goes back to
the mixing bowl. How we cannot expect to be given any clues
to God's great recipe. Follow? And then I picked up my knife,
ready to cut again, and thought, Adel is back in God's kitchen:
there is no call for mourning.

Carl: Alvin, I've told you one hundred times, Adel *attempted*
suicide. She was *not* successful. She is still *alive* and the two of
us have *separated*. Do you understand? Adel lives. Adel lives,
and I am in love with another woman.

Alvin: And I'm glad! I'm happy. I look down at our dirty plates,
some bones and fat left over, some pits from fruit, I look down
at these plates and I say, "God bless us!" Do you know what
I'm getting at, Carl?

Bethany: I feel dizzy. I need to lie down. I'm going to lie down.
(She lies down on the floor, mummylike)

Carl: I'm in love with your wife!

Alvin: I look at these dirty plates, and I think, "God! aren't *we*

5

the dirty plates?" Aren't we the plates who have been taken off the shelf, heaped with little portions of prepared nourishment, eaten off of, finally laid on the table, dirty and waiting to be taken back into the kitchen to be cleaned and what?—used again! and again! The life cycle! Revival! Hope! Divine Design!

Carl: Alvin, I'm in love with your wife, Beth. *I love her.*

Alvin: But of course you love her! It's the most natural thing in the world. What could be more natural? You love her and you love me, and she loves you and she loves me, and I love you both. And before Adel died, we all loved her.

Carl: Adel is alive. I love Beth. I love her and want her. I want to go away with her.

Alvin: I'm not surprised! With Adel gone—though in your grief you temporarily block her burial—you look to new female companionship. What could be more natural? It goes without saying. You see Bethany as surrogate female companionship, am I right? And look—Beth in her beauty and acceptance has sought to duplicate the position of dead Adel. *Look* what she's doing for you Carl. Now how can you say we don't love you?

Bethany: The floor is turning under me. Just me. Your floor is still. My floor is moving.

Alvin: Bethany, would you like another glass of wine? A mint?

Carl: Alvin, I wish you'd just sit still for one minute and try to get all this information straight. (A) I'm in love with Beth and Beth's in love with me; (B) Beth and I have been sleeping together for several *years*—long before I left Adel; and (C) Beth and I want to go away together, live and love together. Is it all clear now? You understand?

Alvin: You love Beth and Beth loves you, you've slept with Beth and Beth's slept with you, you want to go away with Beth and Beth wants to go away with you. I understand.

Bethany: Make something matter. Somebody make something matter.

Carl: Beth, get up off the floor and we'll go away together. Alvin understands.

Bethany: I can't.

Carl: Alvin understands. He says he understands.

Alvin: What's there not to understand?

Bethany: I can't.

Carl: Beth!

Bethany: I can't. I can't get up.

Carl: Let me help you.

Bethany: No!

Carl: Beth! What are you saying? Are you saying you don't want to go away with me? After all this time? After years?

Bethany: I can't get up. I'm stuck.

Carl: Get up!

Alvin: Can I get you a pillow? A blanket, Beth? There's an autumn chill that seeps right in through the floor—not having a basement, the dampness of the earth becomes a problem for us.

Carl: *Beth, get up!* Our plans, think of our plans! The down payments on the cottage, your return to poetry, my new novel!

Alvin: Down payments? Poetry? A new novel?

Carl: Beth! What's wrong with you? Alvin, did you give her something? Did you put something in her wine? Or food?

Alvin: A new novel, Carl? I'm so glad. I thought perhaps with the tragedy of Adel you'd get blocked. You're turning a new leaf?

Carl: Why is she acting so peculiar—did you add something to the food?

Alvin: Carl, I put lots of things in the food. I was at the range all day, mixing things in bowls, adding this and that—all intuitively.

Carl: What is going on here?

Alvin: This afternoon I was out picking the last string beans from the vines. These were late beans—did you think them coarse?

Carl: Beth, what are you doing? Are you turning this into a joke? Adel tried to *kill* herself when she found out about us, and you're turning the whole thing into a joke! Bethany!

Alvin: I stood there among these late vines—late beans—and thought, my God! the glory of nature! I mean, I was picking beans that later that same day we would be consuming.

7

Chewing and eating the same beans that hours previously hung at the mercy of a changing season. You follow? I think the vines thanked me, taking in their children before the autumn chill. I felt blessed, special. When Beth and I moved into this house, I debated the idea of a city garden. All that extra work, I thought. I hadn't foreseen the spiritual feedback. And now *you* have a new leaf, Carl. Tell us about it.

Bethany *(Still recumbent)*: You're a stingy writer, Carl. You have one barely articulated point of view projected on too many thinly disguised characters.

Carl: Bethany!

Bethany: *The Motel of the Heart?* With all those characters? They were really one character, they all had one problem, one point of view.

Carl: What are you saying?

Alvin: Beth's an insightful critic.

Bethany: The character of Georgette? You meant to base her on me. But it wasn't me, Carl. It was you. When Georgette says she doesn't know how to love, that she flies from one set of arms to the next in the desperate hope of finding the right pair, it is you speaking, Carl, your search for the right pair. I lie here, and I say nothing matters. I shout, somebody make something matter! And in your next book, Carl, you'll call me Renata or Thalia, and I'll be standing in a train station; my lover will appear and I, dropping my handbag, my overnight bag, my little wax bag of grapes, will fall into my lover's arms and say—moan—bring me back to life, resurrect me in your house of love.

Carl: What is all this about? Is this a joke, a joke on me?

Alvin: Don't interrupt.

Bethany: I can't tell you the death I feel when I see myself disguised in your books, Carl. When I see you playing me.

Carl: Don't say this! Don't say this! You're torturing me. I love you. I'd never do anything to hurt you.

Bethany: And Adel? Where is Adel now?

Carl: Adel is home!

Alvin: Oh, the perversity of grief!

Bethany: It's you, Carl, you standing in the train station with the bags, with the beaten thesaurus in the overnight bag.

Carl: You're not yourself!

Bethany: Every writer comes to a point of breakthrough. When he sees the lies from the lies, the Georgettes from the Georgettes.

Carl: I love you!

Alvin: You're not well, Carl. The emotional strain. The absence of Adel. Your new book. Too much. Don't you think I noticed how you more or less *pecked* at your food, Carl?

Carl: Bethany!

Bethany: The floor is moving under me. I'm moving.

Carl: You're speaking nonsense deliberately—you're trying to drive me off—you're *testing* me. But I won't be tricked. I'm taking you away, and if you won't get up I'll *pick* you up.

Alvin *(Scraping a plate)*: Carl, you're torturing yourself!

Carl: Beth, I'm going to pick you up and carry you away!

Alvin: You can't pick her up.

Bethany: A weak novelist.

Carl picks Bethany up and carries her like a bride.

Alvin: You're picking her up!

Bethany: I'm being picked up. I'm in the air now, Alvin. There's nothing I can do. I'm being carried away. You'll know I didn't walk out on you.

Carl *(Moving toward the door)*: We're going now.

Bethany and Carl exit.

Alvin: Wait! Wait! I can't believe this. What about the autumn vegetables? What about me? Beth! The pumpkins! Beth, the pumpkins aren't ready yet. Pumpkin pie, pumpkin pancakes, pumpkin seeds—Beth, where are you going? Carl! Beth! Come back! In the spring everything will be in bloom! *(Sits back at his place at the table, considers what has happened)* Well,

that sure took me for a loop. Just whisked her off the floor.
Guess who's left with the dishes? Times like this I think of my
mother and my father. I reconsider them. I think of my
mother, who said, "No matter how well you prepare a meal, no
guest will ever fully appreciate it." And I think of my father,
who, the day after my mother died, thought with a sudden
sense of profound despair as he dropped a frozen pouch into a
pot of boiling water, "I loved that woman, I loved her!"

*Enter Adel. Her hair and clothing are disheveled, her makeup
smudged. Her wrists are thickly wrapped in white gauze.*

Adel: Where is the fucker?!
Alvin: An apparition! Dear God in heaven.
Adel: What? Alvin, it's me, Adel. Where's Carl?
Alvin: Adel! Adel! You're *alive!*
Adel: Of course I'm alive! I'm here, aren't I?
Alvin: I'm in shock, Adel.
Adel: Where's Carl? Carl and Beth?
Alvin: They went away, Adel. You didn't see them? Carl was
     holding Beth.
Adel: Then that was them! I saw somebody with a bundle running
     down the street.
Alvin: That was them.
Adel: Is it too late to catch them?
Alvin: Adel, you're really alive. I thought you were dead.
Adel: That's because Carl wants me dead!
Alvin: Carl said that you were alive.
Adel: Carl wants to kill me, Alvin!
Alvin: No.
Adel: Yes!
Alvin: Carl?
Adel: Yes, Alvin. Carl wants everything in his path dead. He wants
     you dead too, Alvin. He's probably telling Beth right now that
     you're dead.
Alvin: But I'm alive, Adel.

Adel: I know, Alvin, but we're talking about *Carl*. Don't you know who Carl is?

Alvin: I know Carl.

Adel: I hate him! Look at me, Alvin: I'm a mess! And who's made me a mess?

Alvin: Who?

Adel: *Carl!* Don't you know what he's done to me? How he sucked me dry and then tried to bury the evidence? Do you know what I'm talking about, Alvin?

Alvin: No, Adel, I really don't.

Adel: I'm talking about seven years! Seven years with a bloodsucker! You don't think I have scars, Alvin? I have them! I've kept them from people—out of embarrassment and humiliation! I've had to keep my true self down to accommodate Carl.

Alvin: Accommodate Carl?

Adel: Who do you think wrote *The Motel of the Heart?* Carl? Carl can't even spell! I wrote *The Motel of the Heart* and he stole it! Right out of my head!

Alvin: Adel, this is so baffling.

Adel: What's baffling? *(Opening her locket, a kind of pillbox on a chain around her neck, she pops some Valium. This action does not interrupt the lines)* That Carl has used terrorist tactics to publish a novel? You don't know the real Carl, Alvin. You don't know how this sort of man operates! You have any extra Valium in the house?—I'm running low.

Alvin: Adel, I don't have Valium, and I don't think badly of Carl. All people are good at heart, Adel. Even in times of severe strife you must not forget this. I do understand that you must feel a little cut off from things right now, but we can't blame our spouses for our shortcomings, Adel. I'm positive Carl wants to reconcile himself to you, that he still loves you deep in his heart and will share his royalties with you. Carl is very spur-of-the-moment. He and Beth will be back—they've only gone out for a short walk or something. A vacation is all Carl needs. Being a creative artist . . .

11

Adel: Carl is *not* a creative artist! He's a destructive journalist! His novels are no more than a "misconstruance" of the affairs he himself perpetrates on the people around him. Because my love *blinded* me, I have been *duped* into transforming his vile logs into the kindling of fiction. Don't you see the evil? *I'm* the creative one. Alvin! I've been tricked—we've all been manipulated for Carl's personal gain! Don't you see how one by one Carl will attempt to wipe out those who *know*. Don't you see, Alvin, that unless we—the Anti-Carls—mass together we will face extinction! *(Picking up a platter with a cake on it. It has one slice missing)* Pretend this is us, Alvin, our kind— *(A quick sniff)* What is this, cheesecake?—watch me. *(She raises her fist and brings it down violently onto the cake. The cake splatters)* That's what they want to do to us!

Alvin: I don't think God would ever permit such a thing, Adel.

Adel: God has nothing to do with this! You think God cares about bestseller lists and ripped-off wives? Alvin, I am telling you, they want to wipe us out!

Alvin: They? *Who* are you talking about, Adel?

Adel: Carl! You don't think he works alone, do you? Not at this point in his rise to recognition. He has *people!* Hired people! They follow me, Alvin. They know my every move! They followed me here on the bus!

Alvin: You didn't take a taxi?

Adel: I did! They took the bus. *(She is fishing through her pockets and bag. The bag empties itself onto the floor)* Where'd I put my Valium? They must have known I was coming here! You didn't tell anyone, did you?

Alvin: Adel, until a few minutes ago I thought you were dead.

Adel dives under the table to search through her things.

Adel *(Her head bobbing up for a moment)*: That's my point exactly! You don't know the hell I've been living these past weeks. Pure hell! *(She bobs down under again)* If I don't find

my Valium in one minute, I'm going to die right here. Alvin!
Come down and help me!

Alvin descends.

Alvin: Here it is, Adel! I found your Valium.

Adel: That's my lipstick. Keep looking. *(Leaping up)* I found
them! Help me collect this junk. Only two left. I need two. I
had two in the taxi.

Alvin: You need something to drink with that?

Adel: No, I take 'em dry. I've gotten to the point where I can't
depend on a ready water supply.

*They are both off the floor now. Adel is stuffing her things
back into her bag. She remembers her locket.*

Oh Jesus! I forgot my locket!

Alvin: Save those for an emergency, Adel.

Adel: This is an emergency. *(Noticing the leftovers)* What'd you
serve? Is that lamb?

Alvin: Oh Adel, I made—

Adel: Listen to me, Alvin—I'm talking about my life! I came here
to *kill* Carl! How much longer do you think I have, Alvin?
How much longer before Carl gets me? Do you know he
threatened to pull my stitches out? He did! I had to ward him
off with the dogs—Prince and King. The next day he let them
go. He said, "I'm going to release the dogs," as if it was
Bastille Day or something. My only source of protection let out
on the street to be run over. "Why don't you release yourself,
Carl?," I said. "Go stand in front of a truck!"

Alvin: Adel, you don't mean these things!

Adel: Don't I? You know what I have in my pocket, Alvin? Guess!

Alvin: Valium?

Adel: A letter! A letter to Carl!

Alvin: You've written Carl a letter?

Adel: No! It's a letter from a literary society. It came today.

Alvin: You didn't open it, Adel, did you?

Adel: Of course I did! What are you thinking of?! I opened it, and I read it, and do you know what it says? *(Brandishing the letter) The Motel of the Heart* has won some national book award. There's an invitation to a ceremonial banquet!

Alvin: A ceremonial banquet! How marvelous, Adel! A gift from God. I'm so happy for Carl—and for you, Adel. Surely Carl will take you to the banquet.

Adel: Alvin, I think you've been sitting in the kitchen too long. You're not seeing anything clearly! Do you still not know that Carl was sleeping with—fucking with—your wife, Beth? Years he said! Years! Of deception! What do I care about banquets!

Alvin: God, Adel, I would think—

Adel: I'm talking about *Satan*, and you keep bringing up God! I'm telling you, Carl is the maker of all things evil on this planet— all betrayal, mockery, and injustice! *(Banging her elbows, since she hesitates to use her fists, on the table for emphasis. Some glasses may fall over)* Carl must be destroyed! Time is running out! He will take over the world!

Alvin: Adel, I *insist* that you calm down. You're beginning to distort things.

Adel: You mean relax? *Relax.* That's what my doctor says. "Relax, Adel," she says, "relax and stop persecuting yourself with self-analysis. Just relax." *(Picking up a fork and demurely sampling some splattered cake)* Yuck! *(She flings the fork away)* That's too sweet!

Alvin: Beth did the cake.

Adel *(Spitting it out)*: Tastes like poison.

Alvin: It is sweet.

Adel: I don't blame Beth. Though I wrote and typed *The Motel of the Heart* and it was dedicated to her—I don't blame her.

Alvin: Well that's good, Adel. The less blame and animosity you have, the better.

Adel *(Pushing the cake platter aside)*: Alvin, I've been working on a *new* novel. Did you know?

Alvin: No.

Adel: Well I have. An exposé! An exposé novel on Carl.

Alvin: Sounds absorbing, Adel.

Adel: It is. I'm exerting the smallest effort to disguise Carl's identity. Soon the world will see this great minor writer as the forger and bloodsucker he really is!

Alvin: You have the book with you?

Adel: It's in my head. All I have to do is *type* it! I carry all my notes here near my bosom. *(She takes out a small packet of notes)*

Alvin: It's so little, Adel.

Adel: It's in code! And it's going to stay in code until I can find a safe place.

Alvin: A safe place?

Adel: Yes, Alvin!

Alvin: Right before my mother died she said that. She took my hand and said, "Alvin, I'm going to a safe place."

Adel: I need that place, Alvin! *(She leans over to take Alvin's hand and accidently knocks over a decanter of wine. It crashes to the floor. She jumps)* You see! The peril of every moment! Things seeking my destruction! Alvin, I must write my exposé before it's too late—let me move in here—now that Beth's gone, you have lots of room. I won't be any trouble. I'll type real quiet. I'll do the dishes. Say yes, Alvin—save my life!

Alvin: All right, Adel, I listened to you, now have another Valium and listen to me. Carl is good at heart—yes, Adel! Listen to what I have to tell, Adel. Carl may have gone astray, but he is *not* a bad man. He and Beth have probably just gone out for a walk—

Adel attempts an outburst. Alvin cuts her off.

—or maybe they just went away for the weekend—there is no sin in a short holiday.

Adel: Short holiday?! They are fornicating right this minute on some front lawn!

Alvin: Silence, Adel! Listen to me. Perhaps Carl went temporarily insane with the belief of your death.

Adel: Alvin, he didn't believe I was dead—you did. He wants me dead, but he knows I'm not.

Alvin: Adel, listen to me. I'm going to take my car out and bring back Bethany and Carl. Then we'll discuss this all together.

Adel: How are you going to find them?

Alvin: They couldn't have gotten very far. Carl was carrying Beth.

Adel: You're going to bring Carl back? Don't tell him about the letter; let me.

Alvin: Okay, Adel, but you have to promise to calm down, okay?

Adel: Relax. I know, "Relax, Adel." Alvin, before you go, could you get me something?

Alvin: Adel, I told you we have no tranquilizers in the house.

Adel: No. Hot water. Could you bring me a bowl of hot water and a washcloth? And soap.

Alvin: You want to bathe? Why don't you use the bathroom, Adel?

Adel: Don't ask.

Alvin: I'll get it for you. *(He exits)*

Adel *(To herself. Between lines she picks at leftover food with increasing speed and appetite)*:

Carl thinks he's rid of me!

Perhaps Carl will come back.

I don't need Carl!

But I still love Carl!

I should sacrifice myself to a man who is unfaithful, manipulative, and self-centered?

But sometimes he's so gentle and understanding and strong.

You want to be choked by him?

No, but I like when Carl holds me.

Alvin enters quickly with a silver tray on which is a bowl of hot water, a washcloth, and a bar of soap. He places it on the table.

Alvin: Here you are, Adel. Try not to make a puddle. I'll be back as soon as I find them. Now, you're not depressed or anything, are you?

Adel: No.

Alvin: Good. See you in no time.

Alvin exits. Adel washes herself. After some moments Bethany enters, crawling on her hands and knees.

Bethany: Carl is a trap.

Adel, surprised, jumps and drops her bowl of water.

Adel: Beth, is that you?

Bethany: Adel! Adel, you are here! Forgive! Forgive me, Adel!

Adel: You're not with Carl?

Bethany: Carl is a trap! I know that now. He stopped at a phone booth to call his agent and found out about some book award. He started leaping and clapping in the booth and then went on to make over a dozen calls, while he left me lying on the sidewalk. As I was lying there among the dead leaves, I realized what a conceited shithead Carl really is and, more important, how I have transgressed you, Adel.

Adel: Me?

Bethany: When I started to crawl home—I couldn't stand—Carl was still on the phone. He probably doesn't even know that I've left him. Adel, your shoes are all wet.

Adel: I've been bathing.

Bethany: Let me dry them! *(She uses her hair to dry Adel's shoes)*

Adel: Your hair! You don't have to do that, Beth.

Bethany: I want to! I want forgiveness! Will you give it to me, Adel? Will you?

Adel: Does Carl know I'm here?

Bethany *(Wringing her hair)*: Carl is a trap!

Adel *(Avoiding Bethany's grip)*: My whole life has become a trap, Beth! Every day I wake up, and there's a trap. I don't mean just *traps*—I mean *real* traps. I mean, I can't get from my bed to the kitchen without things falling in my path—falling on my head! I try to be careful, I try to take things slowly, watch where I'm going, but—POW! I get it. Glasses fall from the shelves, plates slip from the drainboard, knives unhook from the walls. I touch the toaster and I get electric shock. I make a pot of coffee and it tastes like poison. The kitchen wants to kill me! It's not nine in the A.M. yet, and already I have death on the brain. Do you know what that's like, Beth? Everywhere I turn it's death! I can't get in my tub without thinking death—I think it's a coffin. Death, Beth! I take a shower and I think gas is going to come out. I'm taking sponge baths! Sponge baths over a basin! Why do you think I have my hair all pinned up like this? Because it's dirty! I can't bear to put my head under water!

Bethany: Let me do something for you, Adel. Please let me! What can I do?

Adel: You can—stop hugging my ankles!—you can . . . you can brush my hair.

Bethany: Yes! I can do that! Let me!

Adel *(Removing a brush from her bag)*: I can't stand it—my scalp's driving me crazy.

Bethany kneels behind Adel's chair and begins removing her hairpins and brushing her hair.

Bethany: Do you hate me, Adel?

Adel: I wanted to die when Carl told me he was in love with you. I tried to end myself when he said you'd been . . . sleeping together . . . for so long. *(A knot in her hair)* Ouch!

Bethany: I'm sorry, Adel! I'm sorry!

Adel: Christ, am I itchy!

Bethany: Forgive me!

Adel: I thought you were my friend, Beth!

Bethany: I am, Adel, I am! I don't know what I was thinking of at the time.

Adel: For four years? Ouch!

Bethany: I'm sorry.

Adel: I don't know what it was, but I didn't feel safe anymore. I started suspecting everything. My doctor—she's an idiot—she said, "Adel, don't ever kill yourself without first making your bed and doing all the dishes in the sink." Well, I *never* did those things to begin with. So I fired the maid. Now my bed's an unmade mess and I haven't a clean plate in the house and I'm *still* alive!

Bethany: Adel, I don't love Carl. I don't love him. I don't think I *ever* loved him. I think I only loved the way my body moved beneath his. I think I was loving myself. I never thought of Carl. I'm not thinking of him now.

Adel: Okay, now start styling it.

Bethany: I never loved Carl. I only loved making love to him. I think I realized this when it no longer was a secret, when Carl told Alvin.

Adel: Stop brushing and start styling!

Bethany: You know, Adel, I've never had a orgasm with Alvin. Never. I don't even know if he knows it. Sometimes I think he's oblivious to everything. Living in a world of pots and pans.

Adel: I asked Alvin if I could move in here because I can't stand living at home alone.

Bethany: You don't want to move in here, Adel. You don't know what it's like to live with Alvin. Do you know what he does? He labels everything, puts little gummed stickers on everything with its name on it. As if he's going to forget everything in a minute.

Adel: I hate living alone.

Bethany: We have a girl come in on Fridays to vacuum—Alvin *helps* her!

Adel *(Picking up the silver tray and holding it up like a mirror)*: Oh, Beth. I like what you're doing!

Bethany: Alvin is a terrible lover. He gives silly little chipmunk kisses.

19

Adel *(Holding up a hairpin)*: Here's another pin.

Bethany *(Standing up)*: You know what, Adel? We should go away together, go away and leave everything.

Adel: Go away with you?

Bethany: Yes! What do you need Carl for? Carl was no good for you anyway.

Adel: No good for me?

Bethany: He said you were completely unresponsive.

Adel: Carl said this?

Bethany: He said that you were squeamish.

Adel: Carl told you this?

Bethany: He said that he's always loved you, though.

Adel: Carl said these things to you?

Bethany: Carl is a trap! Let me massage your back. *(She gets up on the table, kneels, and massages Adel's neck, back and shoulders)*

Adel: Carl once told me that I was boring in bed. That's what he says about Zoe in chapter twenty. I want him dead!

Bethany: Where is your tension? Let me massage it.

Adel: Carl used me!

Bethany: Carl is a trap.

Adel: Don't you think I know about traps, Beth? Seven years, and I appear *briefly* in the last chapter of a book which holds *no* interest past the middle—no matter *what* the national book people say!

Bethany: How does this feel? Let me undo these buttons so I can really get in.

Adel: I have something to learn about traps, Beth? A man—and I'm talking about Carl—who in bed called me every possible name—Claudia! Valerie! Laura! Gaby! Zoe! Marsha! Barbara! Amy! Seven years, and never Adel! "Open your eyes, Carl!," I'd shout, "open your eyes and see *who you are fucking!*—I'm not a Zoe or an Amy, I'm an Adel!" Now you, Beth—and I never blamed you—want to tell me about traps? If my mother had lived to see my trap coming, she would have killed herself and then me!

Bethany: Is this working, Adel?

Adel: You want to know who's *really* boring? Carl and his love
novels! And I am *sick* of that love-shit. She loves him, he loves
her, you love them, they love you—love-shit! *(Taking a gulp of
what is left of a glass of wine. Wincing)* What year is this? It's
so bitter!

Bethany: I feel my poetry returning to me.

Adel: That's good. Harder. Easy. Easy. Good. Real good. I'm
coming back to life. "Forgive and relax," my doctor says.
Advice at her rates I don't need. She can go to hell! I'm
writing an exposé novel on *Carl*. You hear me, Beth? I will
reveal each of his cruelties in detail—it'll have to be published
in volumes.

Bethany: Good, Adel!

Adel: Want to collaborate?

Bethany: I must return to poetry. Carl has stunted my muse. To
write I must dip into my well of pain. How deep it is! Carl has
no well and therefore must dip into ours. That's why he's
always hanging over us. Although he doesn't seem to need us,
he does. He sits waiting to dip in.

Adel: I know the well of pain, Beth! I know it. I keep choking, and
I don't know what to do. Every night is the same as the last.
Spiders crawl up onto my bedspread and tell me I'm no good.
They talk to me, Beth! They tell me I'm worthless and should
go die. It's not a nightmare—it's my life.

Bethany: Life is a torture chamber, Adel. I thought of that while
crawling home. Ten men stopped me and offered to put me in
a taxi, and I said no! Let me crawl home, maybe then I'll miss
a few of the flying knives that come out each day to attack us.

Adel: Those are the knives from my kitchen!

Bethany: I'm returning to poetry, Adel. I'm turning my back on
love. I'm turning to the cauldron of art. My muse is back!

Betrayal weighs on me like so much fake jewelry,
Seized by a gloved hand,
It falls like so many unstrung beads on a tiled floor . . .

Look how the lines are coming to me, Adel!

Love is the rack I have been tied to,
A machine of delicate tortures.
My heart on fire seizes the whip
I once cracked under . . .

Adel, listen!

And pushes me, pushes me . . .

(She stands on the table) Adel, the floor is turning! Do you feel it! Under our feet. *(She loses her balance for a moment)* The earth *twists* under our shoes, Adel!

I am the master of my . . .

(Losing her balance again) Adel, hold me! The floor is turning! I can't stand up!

Adel gets on the table with Bethany. They support one another.

Adel: Beth, did you say that Carl has always loved me? He said that? That he's always loved me?
Bethany *(Back to poetry)*:
Betrayal! Betrayal! And vengeance:
The perfume of history.
The noxious scent of coupling . . .

Coupling what, Adel? Help me.

So many lovers falling away like rows of . . . rows of . . .

Adel: Valium. Rows of Valium?
Bethany:
Like so many rows of Valium,
The tiny tombstones of the spirit.

Adel: I like that.

Bethany:
What is love but torture?
The thumbscrews of the heart tightening,
Gripping the half-hopes—

Adel: Carl thinks *he* can write!
Bethany:
—and chokers of disappointment,
The brooch of promises,
That stickpin of the breast
And the mismatched earrings of marriage:
The culprit on top of it.
What is love?

Adel: Torture!
Bethany:
Again: What is love?
Both:
Torture!

Adel *(A tiny voice)*: But I still love Carl.
Bethany:
And men: what are men?

    Tell it, Adel!
Adel: Torture!
Bethany: Again!
Both:
Torture!

Adel *(A tiny voice)*: But I still love Carl.
Bethany:
The weak men and the strong men!
Together they are dust.
So much dust soiling
The apparel of women.
So much filth emerging

From the misguided wombs
Of their unhappy mothers.
What is life?
What is life, Adel?!
Both:
Torture!

Enter Carl.

Adel: Carl!

Bethany: Vengeance!

Carl: Beth, I'm sorry. I guess I made a lot of phone calls. I got carried away by my award.

Bethany: DON'T EVEN TOUCH ME!

Carl: I guess we're a finished chapter.

Bethany (*Throwing a dish of chocolates at Carl*): Eat shit!

Carl: The affair is over, that's obvious. Hello, Adel.

Adel: I came here to kill you, Carl.

Carl: No, you didn't.

Adel: Yes, I did. Didn't I, Beth?

Bethany: Don't trust him—he's a rat with a necktie!

Adel (*Uncertain of her path*): I'm going to kill you, Carl.

Carl: You're not going to kill me or anyone else. You couldn't even kill yourself, Adel.

Adel: He's trying to pull out my stitches! You see!

Carl: Who took you to the hospital, Adel, and sat with you for ten hours until they said you could go home? Who signed the papers of responsibility, so you wouldn't have to spend the night in the hospital?

Adel: My doctor.

Carl: No, Adel. Your doctor was the one who said she wanted to discontinue treatment because your progress was too slow.

Adel: No!

Carl: I'm the one who persuaded her to keep you on.

Adel: You did?

Bethany: LIES!

Carl: Has Beth told you about the award?

Adel (*Taking out the letter*)**:** I have the letter.

Carl: And you came here to deliver it to me. How sweet of you, Adel. And in two weeks, Adel, we'll be able to go to the award banquet, and you'll sit next to me. Maybe you'll be all healed by then. Then we could forget all this. Wouldn't that be nice?

Adel: Home with you?

Bethany: And be killed, Adel? Save yourself!

Adel: I'm writing an exposé on you, Carl. An exposé for the world to read.

Carl: I'll help you with it.

Adel: You won't be very popular after it's published, Carl. You'll be banned in libraries.

Carl: That's good.

Bethany: The table's moving!

Carl: I have the dogs back. I've gotten Prince and King out of the kennel, and they want to see you.

Adel: Prince and King are back?

Bethany: Adel!

Adel: Beth says you don't love me!

Carl: I do.

Bethany: What are you saying, Adel?!

Adel: Beth says you don't want me.

Carl: I do.

Bethany: Stop it! Everything is getting twisted!

Carl: What's twisted, Beth? Explain it.

Bethany: You think I'm Georgette. Georgette, chapters seven through eleven.

Adel: Eight through eleven.

Bethany: We're just characters in your goddamned plagiarized books! Adel—you're Zoe, Zoe in chapter twenty. Shoplifting lingerie in expensive stores. Adel, let us spit on him!

Carl: Bethany, apparently some demon has taken residence in you.

Bethany (*Throwing down a plate*)**:** I won't be a character in a book!

Carl: Try to get some facts straight. (A) My books are fiction. (B) The critics have awarded my book—

Adel: I typed it, Carl.

Carl: —*The Motel of the Heart*—the *best* piece of fiction of the year, and (C) Any similarities to *life* are coincidental.

Adel: A,B,C.

Bethany: BULLSHIT! Crawling through the gutter while you were on the telephone, I realized something: I am not a victim in a novel, I'm a poet! *(Grabbing a flower from the centerpiece)* I WON'T WEAR LOST LOVE LIKE A CORSAGE . . .

Carl: You're really gone, Beth, aren't you?

Bethany: I'm a better writer than you are, Carl. We're all better than you are! You're a *bad* novelist, a *bad* man!

Carl: A poet! How long are you going to go on sending the same five poems to *The New Yorker*, Beth? You think they're amnesiacs?

Bethany *(Spitting out each word)*: I HOPE YOUR BOOKS DON'T SELL!

Carl: Why don't you shut up?

Bethany: You think you're God! A little miniature God—a fraud!

Enter Alvin.

Alvin: I had a visitation.

Adel and Carl: Alvin!

Alvin: I had a visitation. On Park Avenue. I saw God.

Bethany: Alvin, I don't love you anymore. I don't know what love is. I hate love.

Alvin: Beth, you're back.

Carl: Alvin, Adel and I are getting back together.

Adel: What?

Alvin: I saw God standing in a kind of kitchen.

Adel: On Park Avenue?

Alvin: It was indescribable. Sharp knives and forks, a huge cutting board, all kinds of vegetables.

Carl: Alvin, are you all right?

Alvin: Everything's in season. There's no frozen food. It's like paradise.

Adel: What did he say, Alvin? What did God say?

Alvin: He didn't say anything.

Adel: Nothing?

Alvin: God doesn't say anything because he knows all the recipes by heart.

Bethany: I'm dizzy. Dizzy and sick.

Adel: You mean you didn't ask him anything?

Alvin: I didn't, Adel. I didn't ask him anything. I was ashamed. I don't know why, but I was ashamed.

Bethany: I feel the table moving. Slowly. In a circle.

Carl: She's back on that kick again.

Alvin: Look at all the broken things.

Adel: Carl, the apartment wants to kill me. I can't bathe. I can't eat. I can't go in the kitchen.

Bethany: Let's go away, Adel—we'll eat out all the time—we don't need them!

Alvin: Are you in love with Adel?

Carl: Let's go home, Adel, come on.

Adel: Home with you?

Carl: Come on, Adel.

Alvin: You know that I love you, Beth. I love you still.

Bethany (*Pushing things off the sides of the table*): Enough! I've had enough!

Carl: Come on, Adel, I have a taxi waiting outside.

Adel: What should I do, Beth?

Bethany: Adel, don't go.

Alvin: I know now that things are not what they seemed.

Bethany: They're even worse than that, Alvin, they stink!

Carl (*Picking Adel up like a bride*): Adel's coming with me.

Bethany: Adel!

Adel (*Pleading*): Beth, I don't want to be alone, I'm afraid. I don't want to be alone, forgive me. I don't want to be alone, I can't.

Alvin: Something is happening to us. We are being punished.

Bethany: The floor is moving!

Carl: That's because the earth is moving. It's turning on its axis. *(Moving toward the door)* We're going now.

Bethany: The floor is moving!

Alvin: Oh God, say something. I'm so unhappy.

THE END

Slacks and Tops

An old friend writes me from Africa that when you're unhappy in Africa you're ten times happier than when you're in Munich.

Frank Wedekind

CHARACTERS

Constance
Wanda
Edwin
Todd
Ginger

SETTING

A motel room near JFK Airport which dates back to the New York World's Fair with its official colors of aqua and orange. There are many *Vogue* magazines in and out of suitcases.

TIME

Midday, the present.

Wanda *(Talking to herself)*: One night I couldn't sleep and I decided to ask myself what I wanted. I thought I could locate and satisfy my anxiety by speaking to it. I said, Wanda, are you hungry, would you like something to eat? No answer. I said are you horny, Wanda? Do you want to sleep with someone or masturbate? No answer. I said, Wanda, is there someplace you'd like to be—somewhere else in the world you'd rather be? Africa came into my mind. Just like that—Africa. I don't know how long ago this was, months maybe, Africa grew in me like a plant—rubbery and tough—not killable. Sometimes you just want something. You don't know why you want it, you just wake up one morning and have it in your head. When I get to Africa everything is going to make sense for the first time.

Constance, Wanda's daughter, knocks at the door, gets no response, and comes around to the window, where we can see her from the nose up jumping up and down calling "Mommy!" Constance's face is painted white with clown makeup, accentuated with a happy mouth.

Constance: Mommy! Mommy! It's me! Mommy!

Wanda catches a glimpse of the jumping clown and is startled. When Constance knocks at the door again Wanda opens it. Constance is wearing a clown costume, white with colored dots, accordion collar and a pointed hat decorated

33

*with colored pompons. The costume looks homemade.
Constance enters.*

Mother, I need help.

Wanda: Who are you?

Constance: I'm your daughter!

Wanda: You don't look like me.

Constance: This is makeup. Mother, it's me Connie! Are you high?!
I thought I told you to stop smoking.

Wanda: You're Connie! My daughter Connie. Connie, why are you
dressed that way?

Constance: I was going to church. I'm a clown for the church
bazaar—a carnival for children—to raise funds. This is a
costume! Mother, I need help! I don't know what to do with
my life. I can't go back to Todd. I love Ginger but I get
headaches.

Wanda: How did you find out I was here?

Constance: I drove to the house but you weren't there so I went
next door to Mrs. Pincus and she said you were here.

Wanda: She knew I was here?

Constance: Mother, I came here because my life is falling apart. I
can't look my husband in the eye and I don't want my own
daughter to touch me. I feel pushed out of the church—
suddenly it all seems like an excuse for carnivals, luncheons
and bowling tournaments. Todd said all I needed was a
vacation, we went to Puerto Rico. I looked at the buildings
and the sea, then Ginger got sick and wouldn't eat. We stayed
in the hotel room. Just now I was driving to the bazaar and
thought, I can't, I can't face all those children—I was thinking
of myself. Did you know I tried to hurt Ginger? I took her
hands and stuck them in the toaster—deliberately—for no
reason except maybe in some way I was trying to get back at
you and Daddy through myself as Ginger—some kind of
vengeance. Todd made me volunteer for this carnival. He said
it would help me out of myself.

Wanda: She didn't say anything about the police did she? About going to them?

Constance: Ginger? She's asleep in the car.

Wanda: Mrs. Pincus! I'm telling you, Connie, that woman has become a nightmare. It all began so simply: I asked her if she would pick up a few groceries for me. I felt I simply could no longer bring myself to attend another dreary supermarket with all those bunches of women picking things out. She goes every day, what's one more bag to someone who enjoys it?

Constance: What are you talking about, Mother?!

Wanda: I asked her to get me some marijuana and she said no! She said it was illegal. Well, that just isn't true, is it? It's legal, isn't it? It is.

Constance: You're talking in a drug haze.

Wanda: No I'm not.

Constance: Where's Daddy?

Wanda: Your father, Connie, is having an affair with another woman—yes it's true, a girl your age, Connie, younger.

Constance: An affair with a student?

Wanda: That's right! An affair with a student, think of it. I've been deserted, Connie, I'm a shoe in the desert.

Constance: Mother—stop circling me. Sit down and try to make sense of what you're saying. First of all, what are you doing at this motel?

Wanda: You mean I didn't tell you? I'm going to Africa. At last I know exactly what I want. I'd been confused for so many years. I'd been driven by the unnecessaries.

Constance: What are you talking about? Where's Daddy?

Wanda: I've instructed your father to bring me my visa here but I'm not talking to him.

Constance: Mother, we could go back to the house. I have my car here, we could get in it, drive back to the house and you and I could live together again. Wouldn't that be good? I could move back into my old room.

Wanda: Your father says he's sick of everything and that he's going to Africa. He doesn't know that I thought of it first. He's a copycat!

Constance: Mother, I need help! Help me! Todd is going to find out I'm here and come and get me! Mommy! You don't know what he does—he prays for me.

Wanda: Listen to me, you say your life is coming apart? I look to the one who's responsible. He doesn't think I know but I do. He doesn't go where he says he goes. To church? He's not there.

Constance: No?

Wanda: He's with another woman.

Constance: No. What woman? No.

Wanda: I tell you he is! I'm your mother! He is with that girl and right now they are holding one another, they have each other's arms. They've been kissing and carrying on.

Constance: I told you he prays for me. I can't sew—he sews for me. When we were in Puerto Rico I couldn't go out and he sat on my bed and held my hand. When I told him I couldn't breathe with him near me he slept in Ginger's bed. At home he lets me sit still and tells me everything will work out, that everything looks darkest before the light comes. When I open my eyes I see him praying for me.

Wanda: He's praying for you to disappear.

Constance: No, Mommy!

Wanda: I know—I've heard him!

Constance: I should go to church.

Wanda: What for? It's a hive. You'll go there and get stung.

Constance: I came to you because I didn't know where else to go.

Wanda: You don't think I understand you, Connie, but I do. A mother's listening and understanding even when she's not there. Take your hat off, Connie, and kiss me. Kiss your mother. I'm seeing everything clearly: the path we must take. Where is my fan? I have to fan myself. I'll fan you, you'll like that. Listen to me. You think I don't know? Todd is your husband but he feels like a little beetle gnawing away at your life. You love him but you don't love him. His fingers on you at night make you cringe and you sweat and recoil and think you can't breathe. And Ginger is another beetle, a littler one, weighing on you, gnawing. You love her but you don't love her. I know. The church too. A little bell you hear in the distance. Ding ding ding. God. Ding ding ding. God. And the bell every day gets further and further away—ding ding ding—until it sounds like a hollow little shadow of a sound—ding ding ding—and you think it isn't a sound at all but something you're imagining. Take off your collar. *(She removes Constance's accordion collar)*

Constance: I just want to sleep, Mommy, I can't sleep.

Wanda: Do you remember my *Vogues*? I've saved them all. I'm taking them to Africa.

Constance: I left a message for Todd at the church that I was coming here.

Wanda: Oh. Then that was your Todd on the phone.

Constance: He called here?

Wanda: He kept saying "Todd Todd Todd." I didn't know what it meant.

Constance: What did he say?!

Wanda: I hung up. I get so many calls like that. I hung up.

Constance: He's coming for me, Mommy. I just don't want him. I don't want him anymore.

Wanda: Get rid of him. Get rid of that dull boy and come away with your mother to Africa. In Africa you'll be free of everything, Constance. All the gray blurs will become sharp clear colors. You'll know why you have to wake up in the morning. You'll love yourself again.

Constance: Ginger.

Wanda: Ginger too.

Constance: She got sick in Puerto Rico.

Wanda: She won't get sick in Africa.

Constance: I want to speak to my father.

Wanda: Your father's getting ready to leave, Connie. He can't be reached. I don't know where he is. I met your father when I was your age, Connie. How old are you? Your father used to undress me, Connie, so slowly and rub his hands up my legs very tightly and so slowly as if he were putting stockings on me. He seemed so handsome then. And I wanted sex, a sex life. The first times I didn't like it. I felt so sore and bloated. Then when I had you I never felt so sore and bloated in my whole life. I wake up from a nap and I can still feel those hands on me, Connie, those hands on my legs. *(Picking up a hunting rifle)* This is your father's gun, Connie. Hold this gun, Connie. Hold it. Listen to your mother. Close your eyes. Are you listening? Listen to me. A time comes in your life when you stand up and you walk away. Yes. You walk away as if you could feel the wind through your hair again.

Constance: I'm afraid.

Wanda: You'll be very popular in Africa, Connie, people will like you. There's no ugliness or freakishness there, Connie; everyone is magnificent—naked with beautiful bodies. At the airport the people will embrace you, Connie. Every wrong move, false word and wrinkle will be erased. They'll see through all the makeup and the lies; they'll say hello and know you for the first time. Nothing but happiness, Connie. Trees moving under water. Unusual leaves. Giant butterflies. Orchids. Colossal blooms popping their seeds. The pungent aroma. Snakes and cranes, leopards and hyenas.

Constance: I hear something coming around the bushes!

Wanda: What?

Constance: Help me!

Wanda: Raise your rifle—raise it! Do you know what's coming? Do you know? Listen to me!

A man's voice calls out "Constance!" and gives a whistle call.

Constance: No! *(Panicked, she falls to her knees to pray)*

Wanda: Don't you hear it pawing over the gravel? The breathing and the coat brushing against the shrubbery? Get up! Get up on your feet! Don't you hear it—the sharp teeth clicking, the talons tapping, the mouth dripping blood—aim your rifle now! Now!

A knocking at the door, "Constance! Connie!" and the whistle.

It's on the other side of the door. It's waiting to get us. Now! Now before it attacks.

The knocking and whistling stop.

Constance: It went away. It stopped.

Wanda: It's going around to the window. Look! Freeze! Aim! Shoot the thing that has its teeth at your throat! Shoot! Kill it! Shoot it! Shoot!

A tapping at the window. Constance shoots. Glass shatters, two hands crash through the window. Constance screams.

Constance: What have I done?

Enter Edwin carrying several boxes containing his clothes.

Edwin: You've killed your own husband.

Constance: Daddy!

Wanda: What are you doing here?

Edwin: I got a call from her husband. He said he needed a lift over here to get her. Said she took the car and was in a bad way. All he did was talk about you, Connie, how much he loved you and looked forward to you getting better. I couldn't vouch for you getting any better but I agreed to drop him off. Well, I must say, Connie, even for you this was rather a stupid move.

Constance: I didn't do anything!

Edwin: I saw the whole thing from the windshield.

Constance: It was self-defense!

Edwin: I don't recall seeing Todd carry any weapons. Did you think he was going to kiss you to death?

Constance: We thought it was an animal! *(Pointing at Wanda)* She shot him!

Edwin: Oh, Connie, listen to yourself! Your own mother!

Constance: She made me shoot him! *(To Wanda)* Well, you did! I'm innocent!

Edwin: You think that will come out in court? A jury of children would convict you.

Constance: It's your rifle!

Edwin: I registered it and you shot it.

Constance: It was an accident! This is not happening!

Edwin: Not happening? *(He goes over to the corpse, picking it up by the hair)* What's this?

Constance screams.

Constance: What should I do?

Edwin: Wanda, where are my suitcases? I have to pack. *(He empties some of the suitcases of* Vogues *and packs them with his clothing from the boxes)* Now, Constance, if you'd like to go to Africa with your mother and I, carry our bags, we'll consider it. But it means leaving almost immediately. *(Gesturing towards the corpse)* Before Todd's relatives get any wind of this.

Constance: Leave and go to Africa?

Edwin: I'm packing now. *(He is refolding and packing his clothes)*

Wanda: Where's your girlfriend?

Edwin: I have no girlfriend, I have only you.

Wanda: I have my magazines.

Constance: This is just like my childhood with you two talking past me as if I were invisible or not born.

Edwin: Is that so? *(To Wanda)* Why is she dressed like that?

Constance: I was going to church! The church bazaar.

Edwin: It would have to be. If we knew you were going to take this whole church thing so seriously we never would have started you on it.

Constance: You didn't start me on it! I went voluntarily. You and Mommy tried to keep me from going. You told me it was a waste of time and that there was no God. I'll go to the police

myself. I'll tell them it was an accident. I'll tell them it was
self-defense, that it was temporary insanity.

Edwin: They'll have a picnic with you.

Constance: I need a glass of something.

Edwin: Milk? Vodka?

Constance: Yes!

*Edwin pours a tall glass of vodka for Constance. She drinks
it quickly.*

When I was little you wouldn't let me taste your beer.

Edwin: You're mistaken, it was wine we wouldn't let you drink.
You got all the beer you wanted.

Constance: That's because I didn't want beer, I wanted wine.

Edwin: Is that why you were always running off to communion?

Constance: I liked confessing. I hated my life and wanted to say
so. You and Mommy made me feel like dust.

Edwin: And you went to church to get swept? How homey. I just
don't know how Jesus would feel if he knew you were
purifying yourself with straight vodka. Tell me, you think
Ginger will miss her father?

Constance: He used to do her homework.

Edwin: You know, Constance, I'm not saying I wouldn't testify for
you in court—although a little jail might do you good—but,
you know, I really like Todd. I mean I liked him. He wasn't all
that quick, he certainly had odd taste, nevertheless I could
relate to him. And then he liked sports. I like sports too.

Constance: He used to sew my buttons when they fell off. And the
yardwork.

Edwin: That's useful.

Constance: I'm missing a button on my coat.

Edwin: It's a rare man who will sew your buttons when they fall
off. Now when you have buttons and rips where will you go?
Who will you take them to?

Wanda: *Vogue* says time mends everything. *Vogue* says married life
is a come-and-go thing.

Edwin: Well, there you have it.

Constance: I could sit at your feet Daddy and you could talk to me—remember we used to do that? You could tell me what to do and I'll do it—

Edwin: It's a little late in the day for that routine, Connie. I warned you you'd regret marrying Todd but you wouldn't listen and now time proves me correct.

Constance: Mommy, you said you would help me! Do something for me!

Wanda: My parents sent me to Europe: it was a graduation present. In Rome and Paris I sat in restaurants with copies of *Vogue*, flipping through them and ignoring all other girls abroad. They were flat and stupid, wrapped up always in American newspapers. I purchased elaborate shoes and thought how pure life was, how pure and simple without attachments. My shoes, perhaps a flirtatious waiter, the sun setting, my hotel room, a postcard that next morning.

Edwin: How many years ago are you talking about, Wanda? Those cities aren't what you remember. They're desiccated now and they're getting more and more desiccated every day, wake up.

Constance: Mommy. Mommy, Todd saved money for Ginger to go to college—we can use that money to go away—we could go to Paris. Would you like that? I'll do whatever you say there. I'll make you breakfast and bring it to you in bed the way I used to, anything you say.

Edwin: Paris? Nobody wants to go to Paris. It's Africa, Connie, Africa.

Constance: Why Africa?!

Edwin: Don't ask me why Africa. Ask me instead what it is like to sit in the charcoal pit. I cannot describe it. I can say that in a moment too black and horrible to face life with sanity—in this state I sat down in my office chair and heard a voice—a voice so fragile, so delicate and quiet it didn't exist—this voice spoke to me and said, "Go! Go into Africa! Into Africa before it's too late! Go! Go! Go!" I sat up erect in my swivel chair and saw before my eyes—swollen from too many term papers, too many examinations and sour-faced students—before these eyes I saw the golden path of earth's greatest continent. A continent ravaged yet still pure, dark and yet a place of light and hope and renewal, unblemished and beyond question the true paradise of this shriveling and unhappy globe.

Constance: Daddy? Daddy, can I help? I want to help you pack. *(Picking up a shirt)* Should I fold this? Let me fold this.

Edwin: Wanda, you know what I'm afraid of? I'm afraid of overpacking. Leave that.

Constance: I'll be neat.

Wanda: When she'd get home from school all her things were in a little heap on the floor. It didn't matter what she was wearing it went in that heap.

Constance: I always hung up my clothes—you wouldn't give me peace until I did—how could I forget?

Wanda: She's forgotten, but then we haven't seen her in a long time.

Edwin: Constance, you're crushing the one pair of non-permanent-press pants I'm taking.

Wanda *(Smoking the joint she's rolled)*: I think she should sit down and smoke some of this.

Constance: No!

Edwin: Constance is beginning a season of vodka. I knew alcoholism would be in her future. Your mother and I tried to turn you on to pot, we thought it would help your inhibitions—but you wouldn't even try it.

Constance: I didn't want to get high—to live in a hallucinogenic world!

Edwin: A hallucinogenic world! Oh, you're an original!

Constance: I'm not an original! I'm normal! It's you, you two who are strange—who are strangers!

Edwin: Oh, Connie Connie Connie.

Wanda suddenly thrusts an opened Vogue *in the face of Constance, who recoils startled.*

Wanda: Look at this outfit! *(Absorbed again in the magazine)* Of course most of these styles look quite different when you get them home. They don't fit. They pull at you in the wrong places and when you're not looking they turn around and mock you.

Constance: When I was little I thought I was adopted. I was certain of it!

During the following speech Edwin goes into the bathroom and, still talking, comes out with the motel towels to pack.

Edwin: A child's fear of adoption is a common thing, Constance. Why do you always need to see yourself as rare? Why can't you be happy? Why don't you listen to us? Your mother and I both urged to you to attend a college or university—it didn't matter what caliber, we knew your grades were never very high—I don't know why you put up all that resistance. You were so eager to run off and start that family of yours. Now look at you: a young daughter—who knows where she is—your own husband dead on the azalea path, and a clown suit and coat you won't take off. Your problem, Constance, is that you think you're the only one with problems. You're not. This is some sort of syndrome in America. In Africa you don't have children showing up day after day throwing their mismanaged lives in your lap. It's just not done. Perhaps one disarranged life every full moon or so but easily put right by the chief— right, Wanda?

Constance: This is like Puerto Rico. This is just like the room with Todd in Puerto Rico.

Edwin: You're in Queens, Constance, not Puerto Rico and soon we'll all be in Africa and happy.

Wanda: Why is she on the floor? Is she praying again? Stop that praying! It's making me pessimistic.

Edwin: She's just obstinate.

Constance: I'll get married again! I'll get married and I'll go away! I'll get Ginger! I'll go to church! It was only an illusion that God has turned away from me! The path was never shut off from me but only fogged over for a minute!

A jet passes over the motel. Edwin and Wanda look up.

I DON'T WANT TO GO TO AFRICA!

The jet has passed. Constance is on the floor crying.

Why did I come here? Why did I ever leave my home? I killed
the only person who ever loved me.

Edwin: It's exasperating to listen to her! She talks as if her head
were in a bag of steel wool.

Wanda: I don't understand anything she says.

Edwin: Get up, Constance. Get up! Go into the bathroom and flush
some water over yourself, go on. Get! And wash that face off.

Constance exits.

Do you realize what a handicap she's going to be in Africa?
She looks barely able to wipe herself. What is she going to do
when we're living among the wild animals? Do you think she'll
be able to take care of her daughter? I doubt it. We cannot
take that clown with us! Let's not get sentimental, Wanda, and
forget the past! We've tried with that girl—food, clothes,
money! When she insisted on having a wedding didn't we go to
the expense and give her one, even though we both agreed it
was an obscene and imbecilic ritual? What haven't we tried?
What in the name of the philistines hasn't she rebuked? She is
the enemy, Wanda—she has consumed our life, even in her
absence she's always been just a pinprick away, deflating us,
making every dream and aspiration seem absurd and hopeless!

Wanda: When I get to Africa it won't matter that nothing fits
anymore. I'll be able to shed every accessory, every
constricting detail and remembered word, my skin even, even
that. When I get to Africa I will be so naked the slightest
breeze will pass through me. I hate growing old. I thought I
wouldn't mind it and I wouldn't if I had something but I have
nothing and I hate it.

Edwin: Is this jealousy, Wanda? I told you that sophomore meant less than nothing to me! I kicked the girl out of school, didn't I? You're the only one I love. How different do you think that girl—who forced herself on me!—was from Constance? Not very. They're all cut from the same fabric—they'll pick and pick until you've been shredded down to their element. I know—I work with them all day. Every hour students come to my office, students falling beneath their books, telling me they don't know what to do with their lives! There are no answers in a system of constrictions! No longer can I remain a member of the academic community—the community of hypocrites and slack minds! We'll be reconciled there, Wanda, you'll see, we'll be reconciled to everything.

Wanda: I can hear it approaching. It's as if I could part these curtains and suddenly beyond the thin glass see the dark jungle sprinting with naked figures.

Edwin: Wanda, she doesn't want to go to Africa, that's obvious. We've done everything to help her but she won't help herself. She's been a burden since she was born. At least when she was married she was busy. He's not going to be able to keep her busy anymore. She's going to be in our way again, Wanda. She's going to prevent us from going to Africa. That's right, Wanda, she's going to prevent you from going to Africa.

Wanda goes to pick up the rifle.

Don't touch the gun—it has her fingerprints on it. With her fried brains, she'll be tried and acquitted when she'd be better off and happy convicted and executed. Wanda, I got the visas today—that's right, visas and plane tickets—I got them today.

Wanda: Show me the visas.

Edwin: Trust me. You'll see, we'll be reconciled in Africa. We'll be new people, we'll come back to life.

Constance enters. Her face is without makeup.

Constance: Talking about Africa?

Edwin gets down on the floor, doing sit-ups with a rowing motion of the arms and hands. Wanda cuts out clothes from the magazines.

Edwin: I've done this exercise for as long as I can remember. It's kept me in shape. I imagine I'm rowing away from my life. There are times I've had to row longer and faster and times I've laxed up. Right now I feel I'm moving closer and closer. I can sniff Africa in the horizon. I can see under your skirt, Wanda.

Wanda: I care? I'm packing too. I'm cutting out the clothes I like best. They'll be easier to pack and I won't get bored with them. I'll have hundreds to choose from.

Edwin: I can't remember if those people said there was unlimited baggage with limited weight or unlimited weight with limited baggage.

Constance: Mother, Father, I have something to tell you. I forgive you. I forgive you for all the wrong things you've done. I know I've been a good daughter.

Edwin: You don't remember. You used to climb into my closet and slash my shoes with a razor. You used to slash all my shoes. With the same razor you cut the buttons from my suits and coats and threw them from the window. You were too young to remember. I don't hold these things against you.

Constance: I know, Daddy, that you twist things to make me feel guilty. But it's you, you're the one to blame. It's you who shoved me out of the house at seventeen. I was never smart enough. There was always something wrong with me. You didn't love me and you didn't want me to love anyone else. I brought boys home one after another. You didn't even wait for them to get out the door before you ripped them apart. It got so I couldn't get anyone to come to the house: they were afraid. Afraid of being devoured by you and your critical faculties.

Edwin: I have no critical faculties; I never have.

Constance: Somewhere in my head it still mattered to me what you thought and I married Todd because he came closest to what I thought you would approve of. I didn't love Todd but at least he was kind to me. I would have liked a stupider man, Daddy, a man less like you.

Edwin: Todd was stupid.

Constance: You didn't take a leave of absence from the university—you were fired. They said you yelled and hollered and threw things and once threatened someone with a knife.

Edwin: You misinterpret things, Constance, that don't concern you.

Constance: Don't concern me? You're my parents! You gave birth to me! What's wrong with you?!

Wanda: Don't tug at me!

Constance: Afraid Mrs. Pincus might go to the police, Mommy? She said you would sneak into her house and try on her dresses, try on all her clothes! No, Mommy, she didn't call the police—she wouldn't—she said she feels sorry for you—she wants to call a nuthouse. She said she had never in her life seen anyone so out of her mind, Mommy! *(To Edwin)* Do you remember Rochelle? She was a bridesmaid at my wedding. She sure remembers you, Daddy! She said you wouldn't leave her alone. She said at the reception you followed her into the coatroom and pressed yourself against her. She said your pot breath choked her and your hands on her shoulders made her skin crawl. I was a good daughter. You were a bad father and you were a bad mother!

Edwin: You disobeyed us in every way. We didn't force anything on you, we just watched. Watched you sculpt yourself into a simpleton. Constance, I apologize to you for once trying to make you pursue a post–high school education. I was wrong and you were right. You were prophetic actually—to see that everyone would be getting progressively stupider and any information, any intelligence, would be a disadvantage, a discredit. And you, you, Constance, with the foresight of a modern sibyl saw this and sought to keep yourself stupid and I applaud you!

Constance: God in heaven, forgive them. God who is in heaven will not abandon me even if I have temporarily abandoned him, he will not abandon me!

Edwin: That's right, fall back on God. See how far you fall. I've never denied God. I enjoy God. I certainly don't snivel to him. I certainly don't go against the commandments which, as a lawbook, is the whole premise of the Bible, I certainly don't go against those. You know what I'm talking about—I'm talking about husband-killers—I don't do such things and then whine for mercy. I don't do such things and then expect God to do anything but spit on me. You want some fatherly advice? I suggest you go back and read that book more closely. That book the Bible. Because I don't think it sunk in the right way.

Constance: You're evil.

Edwin: Evil? Who's evil? Who as an infant screamed at quarter-hour intervals and in defiance threw things from the crib making them crash against the opposite wall? Who spit up food, crayoned the walls and scraped at the furniture? Who mimicked and repelled the advice of wiser voices around her? Who rejected literature, philosophy and art in favor of organized religion? Who disobeyed the marital advice to stay single until you turn forty, to bear no children—*ever*—and to never hamper your own parents with the lingering burden of believing you still a child? Who? Who? Who then began to propagate, propagate at seventeen? Who? Who disappeared then with her husband into a strange and obsessive commitment to a community church whose own obsession was raising constant capital for extensions and embellishments? Who did these things? Who then after a dissatisfying vacation with the said husband absconded to the side of the abandoned mother and proceeded—*dressed as a clown*—to shoot down the husband in his act of retrieval? Who did these things Constance?

Constance: I didn't do those things.

49

Edwin: You did these things!

Wanda: I've been reading about a tribe. A tribe of people who eliminate the useless and detrimental people in their society by ritual suicide.

Edwin: Con, did you catch all that? *(Taking a rope from around a box, he begins to fashion a noose)* Correct me if I'm wrong but isn't it true that the rope they use for these hangings is made by hand by the villagers from hemp? I'm captivated by this—that they'll just go into the forest and hang themselves—out of a sense of civic pride—for the sake of the whole. Don't you admire that sort of thing? Just for make-believe, you pretend, Constance, that you're that person. Okay? Take the rope and see what it feels like. We'll pretend we're the villagers who've become disgusted with you. Okay, Wanda? We'll call out appropriate jeers to get you going. Is that a good idea? Okay, all together: bad person! Useless thing! Space-taker! Food-eater! Join in with me. Negligent mother! Husband-killer!

Constance: Self-defense! It was self-defense. *(Suddenly she is doing little tricks, juggling colored balls from her pockets and dancing about: bits mashed together from her act for the children's carnival. It is also the tactic of a child attempting to distract her parents from hitting her)* Look! Look! Mommy, Daddy: it's me, Connie! Look—I'm doing tricks—look, "Hello hello hello."

Edwin *(Having made a noose)*: Constance, try on this necklace. It's very chic. Don't you think so Wanda? Don't you think Con should try on her necklace?

Wanda: It's a necklace certain women wear in *Vogue*.

Edwin: That's right, Connie, it's in *Vogue*, put it on.

Wanda *(Holding up a tiny paper blouse)*: It goes with this top.

Edwin: Of course it does! Help her with it.

Wanda: Do you remember when you tried to die, Connie, in seventh grade and we stopped you? You were unpopular in school with the students and the teachers; you were never asked to parties or dates and when you tried to change

yourself everyone laughed at you and called you names? It's
like that now, Connie, it's the same, nothing has changed.

Edwin: You're not a very good mother, Connie. You weren't a good
wife. You're a crybaby and a weakling.

Wanda: You'd rise to the top, Connie—for the first time you'd be
on top.

Edwin: That's right!

Wanda: It would be like going to Africa, Connie, only quicker.

Constance: Ginger. Who'll take care of Ginger?

Edwin: Didn't we make dinner for you every night? Didn't we pack
you lunch in the morning and see that you were bathed? Don't
worry about Ginger. Wanda, fix Constance's necklace.

Wanda *(Easing the noose over her daughter's neck)*: I've got to get
to Africa, Connie—I'm not happy. I'm just not happy. I used
to buy things: scarves, gloves, belts. These were the only
things that brought me happiness. I had a baby and the next
day I bought a sweater with a mink collar. I can remember
holding that sweater up, hugging it and rubbing my face
against the soft fur of the mink. I was so happy! I want to be
happy again.

Edwin *(Tightening the noose)*: Don't worry, Connie, it'll be okay,
we'll say after you shot your husband you got depressed and
hung yourself.

*Together, Edwin and Wanda pull on the rope. Constance
screams, struggles and attempts to free herself.*

Constance: Somebody please help me! I don't want to die! I don't
want to!

Edwin: Well don't expect us to carry you—we're through carrying
you! We're going to Africa!

*Edwin and Wanda abandon Constance, who falls to the floor
crying. Green jungle plants burst the glass windows and
continue to grow wildly into the room. They are joined by the
beating of drums and the cries of animals.*

Constance: I'm going too! I'm going! Todd! Todd! I'm going to Africa!

Edwin: We're going now!

Constance *(Dragging Todd in)*: Todd, we're going to Africa! You can lean on me, Todd! *(Consoling Todd)* It's going to be different, Todd, it's all going to be different—better—better—better.

Wanda *(Collecting her pile of cut-out magazine clothes, some of them fluttering about)*: I'm packed!

Edwin: Africa!

Constance *(Supporting her dead husband)*: Africa!

Wanda: Africa!

Constance: Africa!

Edwin: Africa! Africa! *(He lifts his shirt to expose his chest and his trousers to expose his legs)* Already I can feel the African sun on my body, darkening my skin. Up! Down! Africa in my mouth, Africa on my chest, Africa between my legs, Africa marching in the heat hacking through the green rubber—the lanes of jungle, natives naked with necklaces of teeth! Do you hear it? Africa! Africa! Wild things are calling to us!

Ginger, a little girl, opens the door.

Ginger: Mommy, I can't sleep.

THE END

Christmas on Mars

CHARACTERS

Bruno, 30, good-looking.
Audrey, 27, pretty.
Nissim, 30.
Ingrid, 47, Audrey's mother.

TIME

Act One: July.
Act Two: December.

SETTING

The large main room of an apartment in a city.

The room is completely bare. The walls are painted a very pale
pink. In Act Two the room remains bare except for the addition of
a skirted bassinet.

In the original production of the play, midstage left and right
were two windows. Up center in the room was an archway and
beyond it a hallway running off left and right to the other rooms of
the apartment. Directly up center of the archway was the front
door.

Bruno: I've written a letter to your mother.

Audrey: I hope you're joking.

Bruno: Don't get excited, I wrote her a short harmless little note.

Audrey: What kind of note? Harmless? We're talking about a woman who stuck me with a fork and threatened to pour boiling water over my face. How could you write to her?

Bruno: Listen to me for one second, please, will you? I wrote to her for a very practical reason. Now, first of all, you yourself said you're not frightened of her anymore, right? What happened happened ten years ago, right? And nothing like it's happened since.

Audrey: That's because I ran away from home. You know all this, why should I have to repeat it and suffer?

Bruno: Audrey, I'm the last one to make light of pain from the past, I've had my share but everyone has, everyone's had some bad time at one time or another growing up, but that's the whole point of it.

Audrey: How did you get her address?

Bruno: I wrote her the shortest little note. I said that you and I were in love and looking for an apartment and in fact had found one.

Audrey: This one?

Bruno: That's right.

Audrey: This one? But I only saw it for the first time today. And you told her we found one?

Bruno: But I knew you'd love it and you do, we both do—you

know what this city's like, people kill each other for
apartments—we've got to decide here and now today to take it
or leave it and we can't leave it because I'll tell you, I've been
the only one looking and I haven't found anything this good or
anything half as good or anything really at all else. This is it.
We pay this month's rent, two months' security and sign the
lease by sundown or lose the space completely.

Audrey: You've written to her for a loan?!

Bruno: In a way. Do you think they're going to let us sign a lease
with our skittish income? The landlord works with credit
raters—they want someone with a credit rating and money in
the bank. We need your mother to sign the lease in her name,
yes, and to make a small loan—I have no savings, do you?
This is our chance to move and move quickly. Do you think I
like living with a roommate at my age? And how much could
you enjoy the broom closet you use your entire salary to pay
for? Let's swallow teenage pride, Audrey—you'll feel better for
it—we went out to dinner with my parents, didn't we, even
though they're both hopeless yahoos—it wasn't so awful.
You've spoken on the telephone with your mother a few times,
this is just another step.

Audrey: After all these years of struggling independently I don't
want to ask for her help.

Bruno: You don't have to. You haven't asked, I have. When she
walks in all you have to do is smile, I'll do all the talking.

Audrey: She's coming here now?

Bruno: Yes, to see the apartment and sign the lease and then we'll
have it—we'll have the apartment. We'll move in and be happy
here together.

Audrey: You just assumed I'd like it and want it.

Bruno: You do, don't you? You do.

Audrey: Yes, I do. I do like it.

Bruno: You see, Bruno's not such a bozo, is he? Is he? Am I?

Bruno tickles Audrey. They kiss.

Audrey: There's something I should tell you, Bruno. I've been putting it off for several months.

Bruno: Shoot.

Audrey: I'm having a baby.

Bruno: A baby?

Audrey: That's right, a small one.

Bruno: Our baby, yours and mine?

Audrey *(Rolling her eyes)*: No, mine and the President's.

Bruno: A baby! A baby! *(He laughs, delighted)*

Audrey: Does it make you happy?

Bruno: Happy? I'll say! And how! A baby! Audrey, you aren't joking, are you? No, of course not! A baby! It isn't anything I've thought about but I suppose it's something I've always wanted and thought about without knowing it. A little baby, to hold and play with and dance around. Happy?—I'm ecstatic— of course this means we can marry—we will marry—you'll marry me won't you?—I sound like a fool—Audrey, I love you, will you marry me? Say yes quickly. I love you, we'll be happy, we'll take the apartment, I know we'll be happy.

Audrey: This is the only room that gets any sunlight. I can't imagine sticking a baby in one of those dark small rooms off the hall.

Bruno: This could be the nursery, why not? It's the first room you enter: anyone who would be coming to visit would be coming to see the baby anyway and there it would be when the door swings open. We could put the cradle right here.

Audrey: And we'd take one of the small dark rooms for ourselves?

Bruno: Yes! Why not? We'll be so happy we won't notice.

Audrey: And the rent?

Bruno: Happiness itself will pay the rent!

Audrey *(A joke)*: We can't afford it.

Bruno: That's not true. If I get that cologne commercial my income will triple and you'll probably get a promotion just for recommending me.

Audrey: If, maybe, when and perhaps.

Bruno: Don't be negative, say yes.

Audrey: You've got the job, I know it.

Bruno: Really?

Audrey: Positively. Marian Free told me this morning.

Bruno: Fantastic! And you're to thank I know and I will, on my knees in utter thanksgiving from now until doomsday, say yes, you'll marry me and we'll take the apartment.

Audrey: And you're happy about the baby?

Bruno: Should I do a somersault?

Audrey: I'll marry you.

Bruno: Sound a little more enthusiastic or I'll reconsider.

They have a long kiss. The buzzer rings, they part alarmed.

That must be her—so, everything's cool, right? We're getting married and about to start a new family, a perfect time to make up with your mother, right?

Audrey: I'm not afraid. What difference does it make, I'm adult now. You're right, I should see her, prove to myself she has no power over me anymore.

Bruno: That's right.

A knocking at the door.

Audrey *(Quickly)*: You're not to tell her about the baby—promise me—she'll use it as an excuse to throw herself at me, I know her.

Bruno: Don't worry, I'll do all the talking.

Bruno opens the door. Nissim enters. He is thirty, slightly pudgy, wears an airline steward's uniform and carries a flight bag.

Nissim: Well, here they be, the happy couple.

Audrey: This isn't my mother.

Bruno: Sometimes I think it's mine. What are you doing here, Nissim?

Nissim: Hello, Audrey, that is your name, isn't it? I don't suppose Bruno's told you about me.

Audrey: You're Bruno's roommate. You're an airline steward.

Nissim: That is correct.

Bruno: Nissim, what are you doing here? Please go.

Nissim: I have a very interesting letter with me, Audrey, would you like to see it? It's from Bruno. But perhaps you two composed it together, I don't know.

Bruno: Aren't you supposed to be in Timbuktu or something?

Nissim: I quit.

Bruno: You what?!

Nissim: I quit my job. Tell me, Audrey, how well do you know Bruno, just how well?

Audrey: We're lovers.

Nissim: Oh you think so.

Audrey: We sleep together frequently.

Nissim: I know that! We should start our little talk—Bruno, you may stay or go, it's not consequential—Audrey, you should sit down, what I tell you may shock and disturb you, I don't want to catch you off guard.

Audrey: There's no place to sit.

Bruno: Are you determined thoroughly to play the fool or are you going to leave this apartment now?

Nissim: Well, you can lean against the wall if you need to.

Audrey: What exactly are you talking about?

Nissim: I'm talking about sex—S-E-X, love and sex.

Audrey: Good. Go ahead.

Bruno: Nissim, go home and we'll talk when I get there, all right? We're expecting Audrey's mother any minute and it would make things unnecessarily difficult if you were here.

Nissim: I don't doubt it. I'm talking of things, Audrey, perhaps unfit for a mother's ears.

Audrey: Like what?

Nissim: Isn't it obvious?

Audrey: No, not really. Give me a hint.

Bruno: She's laughing at you, Nissim.

Nissim: Bruno's told you perhaps that Bruno and I have lived together for many years.

Audrey: You were roommates all through college and roommates again after that when you moved to the city.

Nissim: That is correct. Don't you find that a little strange?

Audrey: No. Bruno's led me to believe you've been very dependent upon him.

Nissim: Led you to believe? Oh, Audrey, we don't know each other very well but I'm going to have to call you naive. Well, better you should discover it before the ceremony. Here it is, you asked for it: Bruno and I are lovers.

Bruno *(Shocked, incredulous)*: What? You and I are lovers!

Nissim: And have been since the minute we met.

Audrey: So? Why would I care about a thing like that?

Nissim: Well, you ought to!

Bruno: Nissim!

Audrey: I don't care.

Nissim: Audrey, I don't think you've fully comprehended what I've attempted to reveal to you.

Audrey: You say you two are lovers—great.

Nissim: We do *homosexual* things together!

Audrey: Fine.

Nissim: Don't you maybe see this as an interruption in your relationship that makes it impossible to go on?

Audrey: No, I don't.

Nissim: Well it is! I know no one takes gay people very seriously but this is very serious. I tell you, I'm standing between the two of you.

Audrey: But it doesn't bother me. I had a lesbian attachment once. I had it severed.

Bruno: Satisfied now, Nissim? Go home.

Nissim: Okay, so you're not shocked—

Bruno: Shocked about what? That I nurse a lunatic without remuneration? I'm the one who's shocked. How could you invent such an infantile lie?

Nissim: So, you're not shocked, Audrey, because I have no concrete proof, I understand that and am sympathetic to it so I'm prepared to amend my argument so that I might present tangible documents for that is what you obviously require and here I have them. Letters! *(He has removed a bunch of letters from his flight bag)*

Bruno: What the hell are you doing with those?!

Audrey: Letters?

Nissim: Oh, well, something elicits a response, thank God. Yes, letters! Long feverish letters written perhaps in states of undress. Letters written to your so-called lover Bruno whose real name, by the way, and hasn't he told you, is Elliot—Elliot Frankel! Bruno Ward is a made-up name! Getting shocked? Hard to believe so many letters could arrive at the same address to a made-up name but here they are!

Bruno: I thought this brand of espionage was something only mothers of teenagers practiced.

Nissim: Teenagers? Oh yes, there are more than a few from them. Here's one whose message spills out onto the envelope, "Let's get closer, all risks involved."

Bruno: Give me those!

Nissim: Get away from me—they're for Audrey. Take them, Audrey, take them and commit them to memory.

Bruno: Now we're going to watch you flip out, is that what's next?

Nissim: Planning on renting this apartment together? I'm sure it's not large enough, not for Bruno and all his little friends, his "affairs" or whatever you call it. Here's one from a top model—why not?—encloses a photo of herself in an Italian magazine—this so-called fashion model wants to be a dog— that's a departure that ought to perk you up—according to this letter she runs around her apartment on all fours barking while Bruno holds her leash and pours dried dog food in a bowl. Have you ever noticed the tooth marks on Bruno's ankles? "I fell," he says. Since when do the floors have teeth?

If you can call this an affair I don't know how you can
pretend to know the names of anything. I guess then you can
give everything a new name. I could be a model too if I were a
little younger and better looking—a woman at a party told me
I could be in *GQ*—and she was drinking club soda the whole
time.

Bruno: You could never have been a model. You're too short and
your skin isn't good.

Nissim: That's right, throw that in my face!

Bruno: Why don't you look at yourself realistically?

Nissim: Why don't you die? I am beautiful! I was! And if I'm not
it's because you made me ugly: you not loving me! That's
what's brought me any ugliness I have so you have no right to
say so.

Bruno: Can't you see that you're a nuisance here? Can't you see
Audrey is bored by you?

Nissim: She's in shock! You're in shock, Audrey, aren't you!

Audrey: No, no, actually I'm not.

Nissim *(Rifling through the clutched letters in panic)*: Not shocked
by these?! Read them! Can't you read? "I want you to come in
me until there's no place left to go!" "You are the only one I
love!" "I love you more and more all the time!" "I'm yours!"
"Yours truly!" Look at these letters!

Audrey: Why? What do they prove?

Nissim: That he doesn't love you!

Audrey: If that's true why would he ask me to marry him?

Nissim: That's a question you should ask yourself!

Audrey: Neither of us are virgins. I expected Bruno to—

Nissim: Not Bruno! Elliot! Elliot!

Audrey: Elliot, Bruno, what difference does it make? I expected
him to have had many affairs. Certainly you've had—

Nissim: No, I have not!

Audrey: I'm sure—

Nissim: You're wrong!

Bruno: Now you see what we're dealing with here.

Nissim: No, not completely. There's more to the truth, a simple fact. Bruno's only interested in you to advance his career. Did you hear me? Don't you ever change your expression? He's using you! He's a model and an actor. You work at a commercial casting office, figure it out! When he's through with you he'll drop you like a hot potato!

Pause.

Audrey *(Calmly, to Bruno)*: Is that true?

Bruno: Of course it's not true.

Audrey: There.

Nissim: Oh? This *is* cute! "Is that true?" "Of course it's not true." And that's it. You make a very interesting couple! Don't you care—about *anything?* I see. There's some silent bargain here. Some bargain with lies and compromises. That's what it is, isn't it? I can smell it, the lies. The lies and the compromises. And the doubleness. The perpetual doubleness. Ten years alias Bruno, have it your way, and I are friends and once, once in ten years I'm introduced to his parents. We meet for lunch, it's Easter. I'm told not to be flamboyant, to strive for the subdued. The fact is I'm always subdued! It's only when I have the doubleness to face, the craven doubleness—the hypocrisy—the—the—inscrutable hypocrisy, that's when I become flamboyant. I walked here from across town—walked in shoes a half-size too small and to begin with not designed to walk further than the cab to the doorman—all my shoes are a half-size too small and filled with pain. I wear them deliberately like Christ's thorn hat to remind myself of the doubleness and the falsehood.

Bruno: You sound like a rag doll going mad.

Nissim: You mean a fag? I'm not afraid of being called a fag. Asshole! I choose to be frivolous! Oh God let something frivolous come to my mind! The pain and execution of my feet in these shoes—that is not frivolity! Where is the beauty of the soul? I ask the question and get ridiculed. This century the beauty of the soul has diminished like a shrunken head. *(Throwing down the letters to the floor)* Take your filthy letters! We're through! I hate you! I have driven myself to places of sickness and distraction in the name of love. In the name of understanding I have stopped understanding everything! I have let go of so many things!

Bruno: You hold on to grudges.

Nissim: And you begrudge me that one small luxury! You've granted yourself every possible excess with your dick-crazy girlfriends—me, not even this one tiny concession. I don't dare review the shocking shopping list of predilections these sordid letters reveal lest I gag and expire. *(Spoken at even higher speed)* I will not give up my soul, rather than that I'll give up love—if that's what this is—God knows I've awakened in the night asking myself—tortured again with the duplicity, the malign duplicity of all things and don't ask me what I mean.

Audrey *(Calmly)*: I know what you mean.

Nissim: I've gone beyond it all. I swallow transgression now like water. I wake up in the morning and I feel like a contusion— banged around in the night, blue with the truth.

Bruno: Nissim.

Nissim: Don't even breathe in my direction! As a baby I rolled my eyes behind my lids. I was intolerant of everything, especially of those larger creatures who hovered over my crib and playpen with their fake concern and shrill voices. As an adolescent I sat alone inventing characters for myself—anyone to play with in my misery, making the arabesque connections common only among the insane and gifted: I stunned and isolated my peers, divorced couples flew to my side for advice and comfort, time and again I— *(He faints to the floor)*

Bruno: Well, that put a lid on that.

Audrey: What happened?

Bruno: I thought he was going to tell every episode of his life image by image.

Audrey: Is he okay?

Bruno: He faints like that a lot, whenever he gets excited. It's his

system's way of saying "Enough." I hope you don't believe
everything he says, he's an hysteric.

Audrey has picked up a letter to read.

What's that?

Audrey: It's the letter he walked in with, from you. It says we're
getting married. It was written ten days ago.

Bruno: So?

Audrey: How did you know we were getting married? You just
assumed it?

Bruno: Well we are aren't we? Right? I don't see how the letter
changes anything. I thought he could use the interim to adjust
to the fact, you see how he is about me. I wonder how he got
fired.

Enter Ingrid. She is attractive, forty-seven and nicely dressed.

Ingrid: Hello, Audrey.

Audrey: Hello, Ingrid.

Bruno: Hi, I'm Bruno. Did you have any trouble finding the
building? Well, it's the only one with the awning and it doesn't
really look like the others. Did you notice the little angel faces
on the entablature?

Ingrid: Yes, hard to tell whether they're angels or monkeys.

Bruno: Oh, you're right! But that's the charm of them, don't you
think so?

Ingrid: How've you been, Audrey?

Audrey: Fine. I've been fine. I'm expecting a raise.

Ingrid: Good.

Audrey: Yes, it is good, I like my work and I'm good at it.

Ingrid: Well, you're very smart and pretty and have charm so
there's no reason why you wouldn't be successful at anything
you set your mind to do.

Audrey: Okay, that's enough! We all know why we're all standing here. Bruno's written some kind of letter to you—I know all about it—he's pleaded in some degree or another for a loan and some signatures so that we might secure this apartment. It wasn't my idea—you know better than that. But now that you're here, fine, agree to help or go. If you help we'll pay you back and thank you, if you don't, that's fine too, we'll make other arrangements. I'm just not willing to mystify this meeting into Mother's Day or some such other event of reconciliation. I'm my own woman now and have been for a long time and I'm proud of myself.

Ingrid: Audrey, I just want to—

Audrey: No—don't want to—don't want to anything, because I'm not prepared to deliver and I don't want a scene!

Bruno: Audrey, can't we just take this step by—

Audrey: No, Bruno. Ingrid and I understand each other very well. There's no reason for you to mediate.

Ingrid: Who's that?

Audrey: A friend of Bruno's.

Ingrid: Is he sick?

Bruno: Yes.

Ingrid: He's resting?

Bruno: In a way.

Ingrid: Is he a soldier?

Bruno: A flight attendant.

Ingrid: Isn't there anything we could do for him to make him more comfortable or get him to a doctor?

Bruno: Oh, he'll come to in a minute or so.

Ingrid: Give me a little time, Audrey. Just give me a little time.

Audrey: I don't know what you're talking about.

Ingrid: I want to make up for some things, things from the past.

Audrey: I don't know what you're referring to.

Bruno: Audrey—

Audrey: Shut up, Bruno, I'm talking to Ingrid!

Ingrid (*With difficulty*): I want to patch up the past, Audrey. I want you to say you'll give me half a chance.

Audrey: In other words you're saying you don't want to help us with this little housing problem?

Bruno: Audrey.

Nissim sits up slowly as if from sleep.

Nissim *(Not rushed)*: People think I'm fruity, they don't know my parents were the fruity ones. My mother was a translator and my father an inventor, both frustrated artists—they got into a knife fight and killed each other—drinkers, they tried to instill in me a faithlessness in the future. They called me Nissim—Hebrew for miracles and neither of them Jewish. You must be Audrey's mother. Every Christmas it was the same story with them, "There is no God, there is no Christmas." Cheapskates using ideology as an excuse not to go shopping. After burying my parents I went under the care of two aunts—two complete racists who were in charge of hiring and firing in the city school system. Anything my parents didn't accomplish in the way of screwing me up for life these two hellions finished up but totally.

Ingrid: Hi, I'm Ingrid.

Nissim: Hi.

Ingrid: How are you feeling?

Nissim: Not very well, thank you. Your outfit's pretty but the scarf doesn't go.

Ingrid: I worked once in the garment business and the insignia on your uniform is a lot like the one we used.

Nissim: Really? I was fired.

Bruno: I thought you quit.

Ingrid: Fired? Why?

Nissim: I refused to put ice in the drinks: everything seemed cold enough to me to begin with.

Ingrid: That doesn't seem reason enough to me to let you go.

Nissim: Well, I got airsick.

Ingrid: That could have been from something you ate or maybe you were upset about something.

69

Nissim: I was upset. I got a letter from my friend Bruno that he
was getting married and if he couldn't find an apartment I'd
have to move out so she could move in.

Bruno: Please, is this necessary?

Ingrid: No wonder you were upset. And they fired you for that?

Nissim: I started screaming during takeoff.

Ingrid: Oh.

Nissim (*Holding up an imaginary cigarette between his
fingers*): Do you have a light?

Ingrid: A light? You don't have a cigarette.

Nissim: Oh, I've given up smoking real cigarettes, I smoke these.
I've gotten back to the original impulse for smoking. Light me
up.

*Ingrid lights with a real lighter where Nissim's cigarette would
be. He exhales and "smokes" the cigarette.*

Thanks. I'm glad I'm out of that milieu anyway. Did you know
the stewardesses have sex with the pilots before during and
after takeoff? They all make the same fake motor sounds when
they come. The stewards work twice as hard as the
stewardesses because they all wanted to be stewardesses in the
first place. The food's not half-bad.

Bruno: Ingrid, why not take a look around the apartment.
Through that door there's a corridor which leads to some
other rooms. The layout's kind of wonderful. It's an old
building, in great shape and with lots of character.

Ingrid: It's nice. I like it. The other rooms are through here?

Bruno: That's right. Take a look. It's very special.

Ingrid exits to inspect the other rooms.

Okay, are you going to leave now or am I going to kick you
out?

Nissim: I'm not the one who wants to be a dog so don't talk to me
as if I were one.

Bruno: If you make yourself into a ludicrous thing how else can I talk to you?

Nissim: Where are you going to find someone like me who cooks for you?

Bruno: I don't exactly call mixing yogurt with a tablespoon of instant coffee cooking.

Nissim *(To Audrey, desperately)***:** It was in a recipe book and it tastes like parfait!

Audrey: I do it.

Nissim: Audrey, do you think I'm too fat or too skinny? I try to lose weight to look slender, then I think I'm too puny and I try to gain weight. In an effort to overcome shyness I become grotesquely friendly. I've stopped looking at people. I don't know who's flirting and who's looking in utter disbelief.

Audrey: I'm sorry, I was thinking of something else, what was the question?

Bruno: The question is how long are you going to stay a flippo? Don't you see it's your way of not growing up and being a man?

Nissim: And you—how long will you still rely on your pathetic little career to buoy you up?

Bruno: Oh, go faint! Audrey, listen to me, let's play this right, okay? The only reason to have your mother here at all was to get her help not to frighten her off.

Nissim: You're very busy in the gym with your weights—why not build up your character, that's the really scrawny side of you. My aunts and parents were lunatics but at least I know up from down.

Ingrid enters.

Ingrid: The dark rooms off the hall could be a problem but it's not a bad apartment. When you take into account the size and the way these buildings have appreciated in the last few years, I would even say the price is fair.

Bruno: I'm so glad you like it! I was so excited when I found it. I called Audrey at the office and insisted she zoom right over. As you say, finding an apartment like this in the current market is a minor miracle.

Nissim has taken out several sandwiches, a small jar of mayonnaise and a knife to spread it with from his bag. He eats a sandwich.

Nissim *(To Ingrid and Audrey)*: Sandwich? Sandwich?

Ingrid: No, thanks.

Nissim: Do you have an ashtray?

Ingrid: No. *(As a second thought looking through her handbag and removing a sea shell)* Will this do? It's a shell.

Nissim: Oh, I don't want to use that, it's too good, doesn't it have sentimental value?

Ingrid: I don't want it to anymore. Please, use it.

Nissim: Thank you. Sure you don't want a bite? No-cal mayo. I have six snacks a day and then I take these appetite suppressants.

Bruno: If you're not going to go, please stop talking.

Nissim: It's easy for those without appetite to mock the hungry.

Ingrid: I've felt that too.

Nissim: I'm a physicist really—I graduated as a physicist in college.

Bruno: You did not. You never even graduated.

Nissim: So I dropped out the month before graduation, what difference does that make? I was an honor student. The dean had me on his list.

Bruno: Ten minutes ago you said you were going to be a model, now you're a physicist.

Nissim: So? Brains and beauty can't go together in your mind?

Bruno: They can but you're not particularly brainy or beautiful.

Nissim: I need this?

Ingrid: You two sound like an old married couple.

Bruno: Yeah, well, you know, old friends are like old couples.

Ingrid: I do like this apartment. A lot.

Nissim: I like it too. And I'll be needing a place.

Bruno: What?

Nissim: The old one will remind me of us.

Bruno: What us, there is no us! Ingrid, please ignore this person. He's been trying to pass himself off as something more than my burden in order to prevent Audrey and me from marrying. You know, it's one of those friendships you make when you're too young to know better and then spend the rest of your life trying to shake.

Ingrid: I like him.

Bruno *(An about-face)*: He's my best friend, I'm not saying anything bad. I'm just trying to make everything clear so you get the right picture.

Ingrid, on cue with Nissim, who barely indicates he is about to have another "cigarette," gives him a light.

Nissim: The right picture, Ingrid, is these two don't care a button for each other but think they do or want to think they do or something even more insidious I'm too pooped to imagine.

Ingrid: Audrey, is this true? Are you just marrying for no reason? Are you in love?

Audrey: What's it to you?

Ingrid: You're my daughter. I love you.

Audrey *(Violent)*: Oh, please! Won't you spare me?!

Bruno: We do love each other, of course! What other possible reason nowadays would provoke two people to marry? We are in love. We love each other.

Audrey: My mother's a very practical person, Bruno. She'll appreciate and understand us for speaking more directly to her.

Bruno: What do you mean?

Audrey: Oh, why pretend anymore, Bruno? It is rather silly, all this the sky is blue and I love you—better we should drop it now, as Nissim says, before the ceremony. Let's admit that when we sign the contract we're doing just that—signing a

73

contract. She's not going to help us, can't you see she's thinking of getting the apartment for herself?

Ingrid: If this is honestly the way you feel, Audrey, you shouldn't be marrying.

Audrey: Oh no? Why? How big a difference will it make from your marriage, the one that lasted two weeks, the one with my father? Were you so in love?

Ingrid: No, obviously we were not. We were friends.

Audrey: Oh, friends. Well, Bruno and I are friends too.

Bruno: We're more than friends, Audrey, what are you trying to do?

Audrey: Please, Bruno, I'm talking to Ingrid now.

Bruno: So I've disappeared? You're just trying to drive her off!

Nissim *(Holding up half a sandwich)*: A half?

Audrey: Bruno and I understand one another. We're a lot alike, I knew that the minute I met him. I expect our marriage to last more than two weeks, two years, two hundred years, what difference does it make to you?

Ingrid: Audrey, I never married your father, I made that up. We were friends, and I wanted a baby so we had one. He met some woman and went off and married her.

Audrey *(Frightened, violent)*: Do you think I want to hear this now?

Ingrid: So we tipped our hats or whatever we had on our heads at the time and said so long. He was not interested in having children. At the time I didn't think that was the best cradle talk so I weaved a tale of divorce—it was the best I could come up with at the time—there was no divorce, it was invented for your benefit, Audrey, to make you feel less lonely and have more to tell your friends when asked where your father was. I didn't think it would turn on me and you would grow to hate me.

Audrey: Liar.

Ingrid *(Takes a letter out of her bag)*: When you were a baby I wrote to your father that he should at least visit you at holidays and set up some form of communication and he wrote back this letter. Take it, it's all made very clear. Read it.

Audrey: An old letter. Oh, this is good! What does it say, that he didn't care to see me? You've told me as much, what do I need to read? Isn't this convenient? It seems today everyone has a letter of some kind to produce at some key point and foul up other people's lives, some nasty and concise little letter. Keep it! You've kept it this long, keep it, I don't want it.

Ingrid: Take the goddamn letter, Audrey! I won't be blamed for your father anymore—you hate him? Go to him with it, seek him out, the return address is on the envelope—it hasn't changed, stalk his building, attack his wife, defame him, scar him if you can but please forgive me at last won't you, can't you?

Audrey gingerly takes the letter, holds, doesn't open it.

Audrey: Are you stupid? Do you think you're going to walk in here with some yellowed prop from the past, distort the truth and reinstate yourself in a role you can't possibly have? You'd have been better off signing the lease and bribing us with the security deposit. Now get out!

Bruno: Audrey, you're really overdoing it.

Audrey: Shut up!

Ingrid: Please, Audrey.

Audrey: Get out! You didn't want me as a baby and I don't want you now: get out!

Ingrid: Who said I didn't want you? I did. I did always. Give me a chance, Audrey—if I was a bad mother give me a chance to be a better one—I'm begging you!

Audrey: Don't touch me! *(She rips up the letter violently)* Don't you dare touch me! Do you really think I'm going to let you have another chance at me?

Ingrid: Audrey, please, I love you.

Audrey screams as if hot oil has been thrown upon her and exits running to the corridor and bathroom.

Nissim *(After a pause)*: Maybe I should go after her and help her. I have some onboard fresheners with me and a comb. *(He remains on the floor)*

Bruno: Maybe this wasn't such a good idea after all, you coming here. I didn't realize she'd be so . . . I guess people don't ever recover from things like child abuse.

Ingrid: Child abuse? What do you mean?

Bruno: I mean Audrey's told me how things were with you growing up. I'm not here to pass judgment. I'm just saying it must not be easy to recover from those kinds of scars.

Ingrid: What has she told you?

Bruno: Oh, there's no reason to list the things here and embarrass one another, you know what they are.

Ingrid: Tell me. Tell me what she told you.

Bruno: What, is this guilt-and-punishment day? You know what things you did! Beating her with an electrical cord, sticking her with a fork, pouring boiling water over her head.

Ingrid: She told you I did these things?

Bruno: Well you did! Didn't you?

Ingrid: No. Never. I've never hit Audrey. I've never even shouted at her.

Bruno: I don't understand. She told me the whole time she was growing up you beat her with objects until she couldn't stand it anymore and ran away from home.

Ingrid: No.

Nissim: You mean it's not true? She made it up?

Pause. Ingrid doesn't answer. She's obviously in great turmoil, wanting to speak, unable to speak. Pain, shame and anger rising conflicted to the surface, it shows in her face and speech: she loses her warm and cool composure and comes apart.

Ingrid: No, I never hit her. Something worse. It's worse. So much worse. I'm so ashamed, oh God! I feel so low, so low for so long, I can't stand up.

Nissim *(So softly)*: What happened?

Ingrid *(A pipe bursting)*: I fell in love! *(Drowning)* I fell in love, I fell in love. With a man. A man appeared. I'd never believed in love like that, to be taken up like that and be erased completely. I forgot my name. I only knew I loved him and would walk into fire for him. He was jealous. Didn't believe Audrey's father wasn't a lover. He never said so but I think he resented Audrey. *(Gagging)* He hated her. He wanted me to go away with him. Audrey was just a little girl at the time. I left her with my sister. It was temporary I thought. Today is the first time I've seen her since.

Nissim *(Softly)*: What happened to the man?

Ingrid: What? What happened? Look at me. Look at my face!

Bruno: I should check in on Audrey, see if she's all right. *(He doesn't move)*

Ingrid: I had a business at the time, another business. He made fun of it and borrowed money from it, not to gamble or anything like that but to supposedly live better. He was sort of a philosopher. He didn't work. I neglected the business, it fell apart at both ends, the money ran out. We began to fight all the time. This is ridiculous to tell. And then he left me. It's ridiculous!

She stops to cover her face, crying, half-laughing at herself. She is a little bit frightening. Nissim hands her a tissue.

I couldn't get up! An old woman who lived at the hotel I was staying at came in twice a day to feed me. I couldn't even clean myself. I sat all day in a chair near the door with my suitcase like a dead person. At night I made phone calls. I talked to myself. People hung up on me. I cried so much I couldn't breathe. I wanted to die! I'd left my child for this man.

Bruno: What did you do?

Ingrid: I made a lot of money. It seemed like the only alternative, that or die. I started another business.

Nissim: A few years ago I hypnotized myself into believing I was a bisexual or something and I married a girl. She was a junkie. We were happy briefly I think. She disappeared eventually but not before we attempted to adopt a child. It was the whole reason we came together, to enhance our chances of getting through the initial application period. They told us there was a paucity and when we pressed them further they sent us runaway teenagers, you know, that city program where you keep them in your home until they remove everything with any resale value and then run away again. I taught kindergarten for six months. I wanted all the children to love one another but every day it got more and more obvious they would grow up to be criminals like their parents. *(He rises from the floor)* I'm going to help Audrey. It's my job. Ingrid, if you go out for anything I need another pack of cigarettes. And don't get them in the lobby the price is inflated.

Bruno: What difference does it make where she doesn't get them as long as they're imaginary?

Nissim: That's no reason to get gyped. *(He exits)*

Ingrid: He's in love with you, you know.

Bruno: I know, my cross to bear. I've been his support system for the last ten years! True, there was a brief respite when he married that fellow maniac. Next to her he seemed like the rock of ages. Stoned and haywire. In one of her less aphasic hours she ranted to me how I was responsible for the way Nissim was and therefore he was my responsibility. Do you think that's so? I don't really think anyone's really responsible for really anyone. It's true I became friends with Nissim out of maybe a spurt of vanity, knowing I could by association make even a misfit like Nissim an insider. Colleges are like that. Actually, the whole world is like that. I've always been good-looking and traded upon it. Do you find me good-looking? When I was a baby my mother told me I looked like a munchkin and that my brothers were better-looking. My mother has this theory that if you're good-looking you can get anything you want out of the world and if you're not you can expect nothing. The idea sounds grotesque but

experience seems to confirm its truth. My father manufactured
sports equipment for children. That's how I got started. I hit
balls with bats, threw them into hoops and kicked them toward
end zones, in black-and-white and then in color. I was the only
kid on my block with an income. I was despised and idolized. My
brothers thought it too sissified to model. Anyway, as they grew
up they got more and more horselike. They're partners now and
sell pharmaceuticals. We don't communicate. You're very pretty,
actually, prettier in a lot of ways than Audrey. My hair's not as
thick as it used to be. There's a thickness under my eyes and a
spider of lines near my mouth. My parents were good-looking, in
a way, but cruel and stupid also. As they've gotten older they've
lost their looks and have become jolly and inoffensive.

*Ingrid has picked up a handful of the letters strewn on the
floor and reads aloud at random with no intonation, as if
reading a foreign language with good to average skill.*

Ingrid: "It's night now, my husband's asleep in the other
room. When he touched me before I shut my eyes and
pretended it was you and trembled. Are you thinking of me
now, Darling?" "You asked me to send this, with it I send my
arms, lips and tongue, kiss this letter after you read it—I'll
feel it down here. Until I see you I remain your love slave in
escrow." "When you talk to me in bed it ends the unbearable
silence of existence."

Bruno: I thought it might be exciting to reread the letters long
after parting company, to give myself a rise when my hair goes
white. And this shell? It's that guy's, isn't it, your lover?
Something you found together on the beach, right? Or
something you picked up as a reminder the day you decided
you'd cried enough and weren't going to cry anymore. And at
night when you feel weak you hold it up to your ear and cry
anyway because it reminds you of the sea, but really the sound
it's just air, right? *(Holding the letters and the shell, he opens
the window)* Who needs them, right?

79

He throws them out. The shell falls silently away and the letters, caught by some wind, fly up and away before he shuts the window again.

Ingrid: Hold me. Hold me. Please. Just for a moment. Please hold me. I'm so lonely. Lonelysick down into my guts. Just for a moment. Hold me.

Bruno embraces Ingrid. He kisses her on the mouth. She shudders and weeps.

Bruno: What's wrong? Don't worry about Audrey, she'll come around. You'll see, the baby's going to make all the difference in the world.
Ingrid: What did you say?
Bruno: I said once the baby arrives everything will be—
Ingrid (*Seeing the first ray of light after years of darkness*): Say it again!
Bruno: What, that Audrey and I are having—

Ingrid falls to her knees at Bruno's feet.

Ingrid: Please, please.
Bruno: What's wrong?
Ingrid: I'm willing to do anything, anything.
Bruno: What's got into you?
Ingrid: All I want is a part, just a part.
Bruno: A part? A part of what?
Ingrid (*Faster than her regular speaking*): I did such a botch-up job with Audrey, she'll never forgive me and why should she. I'll take the tiniest and darkest room off the hall, you won't even know I'm living here I'll be so quiet and invisible. All I ask is that I be allowed near it, to hold it and kiss it because I love it already, I do, I love it with all my heart and I want more than anything to feel my heart again, to feel something— I want to feel joy! In exchange, in exchange I'll of course pay

for the apartment, I'll pay all the rent, the utilities, the furniture, anything—Audrey will have to take off from work—I'll supplement her salary and wait on her—you can take fewer jobs, pick and choose the ones you like, quit altogether if you like—this is the chance I've been looking for, the chance to live again!

Audrey and Nissim enter hand in hand.

Nissim: Audrey and I have exchanged face-washing techniques and have become fast friends.

Audrey *(To Bruno)*: Why is she on her knees?

Nissim: You can get up now, Ingrid, Audrey forgives you.

Audrey: I didn't say that I—

Nissim: No! Audrey, now! What did I tell you in the toilet? To say you forgive is three-quarters of forgiving.

Audrey: But I didn't agree with you.

Nissim: Hush! To forgive is to be at one with the season of rebirth. Don't you want to be at one with spring?

Bruno: It's July.

Audrey *(To Bruno)*: You told her didn't you? You told her.

Nissim: Told her what? Where did my ashtray go?

Ingrid *(Still on her knees)*: Audrey, I want to help. I want to make up. I'll do anything you want, I'll be anything, just don't shut me out, not now, not at this time.

Nissim: What time? What does she mean "this time"?

Audrey: Nissim, I didn't tell you in the bathroom but I'm pregnant.

Nissim: A baby. A baby? Not a little baby, a little thing, a baby, no.

Audrey: Yes.

Nissim: A baby. But, Bruno, is this true, your baby? Tell me Bruno, your baby?

Bruno: Yes! Yes, Nissim!

Nissim: A baby! *(He falls to his knees to pray)* Oh merciful God who has taken this time to shed light on this miserable and thirsty soul, one thousand thank-yous, from this day on I walk in a state of gratefulness and if I should stray from gratitude please kill me in my path, I love you so, yours, Nissim.

Audrey: The baby is mine. It belongs to me.

Nissim: Tell her, Bruno. Tell her. Bruno, tell her.

Bruno: Tell her what?!

Nissim: About the baby, your first baby. About the knife, tell her.

Bruno: I don't know what you're talking about.

Nissim: Oh no? Look everyone, look! *(He opens his shirt and reveals a gash with stitches)* My scar—twenty-four stitches. How did I get twenty-four stitches and not very far from my heart? Seven years ago May fourth Bruno and Nissim go out for ice cream—out from the bushes springs a devil, hissing for money! We hand over our wallets, "Good evening, Unkind Sir, do have a sporting time somewhere with our money, bye." *"I want those watches! Give me those watches!"* We hand over the watches, lose what time we may, he got the watches. Not enough, he spots Bruno's ring and says, *"Hand it over!"* "No," shouts Bruno. "No!" Well, no apparently is the magic word. *"No? No?"* Out comes the knife ready to cut Bruno's face. I throw myself between Bruno and the knife, holding my own knife, my mayonnaise knife. His knife cuts my chest, my knife cuts nothing but we all run into the night on our own. At home Bruno says he will give me anything in repay, for saving him. Twenty-four stitches and nearly I lost my life! Promise me your firstborn.

Bruno: Enough! When eccentricity dances over into the certifiably insane it's got to be put a stop to!

Nissim: You promised me!

Bruno: Well, I didn't mean it! I meant it as a form of speech, as a hyperbole for my gratitude. I never even expected to ever have a child.

Nissim: It's mine. The baby is mine. I earned it. It's promised to me. I'm sorry, Audrey, I'll make it up to you.

Bruno: He thinks he's Rumpelstiltskin! You're a nut! A nut! A hopelessly cracked nut!

Nissim: I am not a nut. I am inviolate and holy. The baby is mine! Mine!

Bruno: Is this going to be another fit scene, Nissim? Isn't it someone else's turn?

Nissim: I'm sorry, Audrey, try and understand me—what my life has been like—I wasn't cut out for it—I'm too pure—it's all too sordid, the world—I can't go on without it, without the baby—when every magazine ad mocks me, every TV plot and commercial, every store window telling me what I want is not normal, is not a romance, is upside down and warped and then, as if all this treachery heaped on me were not enough—I have *him* who embellishes every day with still another betrayal, another degrading episode recorded in letters. What sin in the name of sexual contact haven't you committed—have you even read your own letters? Where are they? Where'd they go?

Bruno: You're just repressed, Nissim, that's why you're so easily derailed by things which wouldn't upset a twelve-year-old.

Nissim: I'm repressed? You're the most repressed person I know! What's more repressed than promiscuity?

Bruno: Won't you ever get tired of jabbering?

Nissim: No, only of the lies, villain! The baby is mine!

Bruno: Stop saying that!

Nissim: The baby is mine. My soul is in that baby.

Bruno: Well get your soul out of it but quick!

Nissim *(Resolute)*: It's my baby. I'm having a baby.

Bruno: If there was a phone here we'd dial it and have you taken away.

Nissim: Take me away, you've taken everything else from me—what haven't you taken? Tell them, Bruno, how you come into my room and steal everything.

Bruno: I never stole anything from you.

Nissim: Nothing tangible—but nothing valuable ever is. I broke all your mother's dishes, Bruno—I did.

Bruno: What!

Nissim *(To Audrey and Ingrid)*: They had a Birds of Paradise pattern on them and for years those birds have been mocking me, squeaking up from the soup or salad, "You'll never get to paradise." I couldn't take it anymore and I smashed each one against the wall. If there's no paradise how can I go on? How can I wake up and face all the animals in this zoo?

Bruno: I'm going to break you in half!

Nissim takes out his sandwich knife and holds it up.

Nissim: Stay away from me! I can wield a knife too you know! Who wants to be cut first?

Ingrid: Nissim, you can visit the baby whenever you like, you can be the godfather, that would be good.

Nissim: I've grown so sick of musty reassurances—I've had so many! For kindness I've had to sink and sink and sink! I'm sick of kindness, of tiny kindnesses taking up space nibbling at everything and leaving me starving.

Bruno: Put the knife down, Nissim. Put it down.

Nissim: You will have to kill me before I forsake it! Better I should die at my own hand than waste away from despair!

Audrey feels, for the first time, a movement from the baby. She is alarmed and excited and lets out a sound.

Audrey: I feel it! I feel it, the baby.

Nissim, shocked and alarmed, also touches his stomach, feeling a sympathy pain. He lets out a sound and faints.

Bruno: Here we go again.

Curtain.

END OF ACT ONE

ACT TWO

Five-and-a-half months later.

Bruno: Can this go on? No, not really, not if you think about it
for more than five minutes. Your mother being here half
makes sense—she's supporting us and she'll be able to help
with the baby. But him? How many babies can we nurse at one
time? And he's going to be a bad influence on that baby, that's
a fact. We can fool ourselves into thinking otherwise but let's
face it: he's emotionally unstable, overneedy, overbearing,
hyperactive, talkative. I mean sit down and really ask yourself
do you want a son or daughter who acts like him? No, of
course not. And we can't afford him. He brings in no income.
You're not working anymore, I'm working less frequently now.
Your mother's made some remarks about expenses suggesting
there's a limit to what she has in that account. We just can't
afford the extra mouth to feed! On top of all this, and you
know this, he loves me. Think what that's like for me, Audrey,
the strain of it. Before at least the admissions were repressed
and avoidable but now that he thinks *he's* having the baby he
thinks we're all married to each other! He's having a bad
effect on you too, Audrey. I know you're not fond of this topic
lately but *when are we going to get married?* I'm not
complaining, not at all, I know it must be a big strain to carry
around a developing baby for nine months—more than nine
months, the doctor says you're drastically overdue—and that a
man can't begin to imagine what it must be like but I don't

think it's so much the baby that's come between the intimacy between the two of us, but him. You know what I'm talking about. Should I get you a chair? I can get you a chair.

Audrey: No.

Bruno: I'm talking about us making love—you don't want to do it anymore and you won't talk about it and I know why, this is some offshoot of his whole celibacy-trip isn't it? The doctor says there's nothing wrong with intercourse during pregnancy so what's the problem? The problem is him, him right down the line because he's moved in here and more or less taken over your mind. You don't listen to me. You don't listen to your obstetrician. You listen to him, the doctor of hysteria. Can't you see he's on the fast track to nowhere? We can't sit down and plan our lives with a tag-along, it makes happiness a complete impossibility but happiness—and can't you see this?—is anathema to him! He's happy unhappy! Have you ever seen him make any attempts to meet anyone, to find someone? We can't have him preying upon our lives indefinitely—he can visit anytime—we said he could be godfather—what else could he expect? Today we tell him. Do you understand? Before the baby arrives I want him out!

Nissim (*Offstage, jubilant*): Everyone close your eyes, I'm coming in.

Bruno: We're not closing our eyes so just come in.

Nissim enters with shopping bags, packages, and a beautiful, real, evergreen tree.

Nissim: Isn't it the most beautiful, the most perfect tree? I hunted like a maniac and then suddenly just as it was getting dark, this one reached out and picked me. This is the first year I wasn't too depressed to go tree-shopping. Usually I skip it altogether or attach some branches and a star to the TV antenna. Smell the tree, Audrey.

Bruno: Nissim, Audrey and I have been having a little talk.

Nissim: I bet I know what you've been talking about.

Bruno: I bet you don't.

Nissim gives Audrey a bag of chestnuts. She eats them.

Nissim: I brought you those chestnuts. Have you had your nap yet? Did you eat the lunch I left you? How are you feeling? Do you think you might have it today? Bruno, you were going to get out the tree stuff while I was gone.

Bruno: Nissim, I'm bringing a chair in here. Audrey wants to sit.

Audrey *(Eating chestnuts)*: I don't want to sit.

Bruno: Well maybe I want to sit! This chairlessness is ridiculous!

Nissim: Bruno, please, let it pass one day without this argument.

Bruno exits.

I saw Marian Free shopping this morning. She sends her regards, says she'll never forgive you for not attending your baby shower and wasn't going to mail you the presents but did anyway and not to expect them right away because she didn't send them first class. I made up a good reason why you weren't seeing anyone and that it wasn't personal or anything.

Audrey: Bruno says you'll be a bad influence on the baby, that we can't afford to keep you, that you're having a bad effect on me and that he wants you out.

Not moving, Nissim considers these things for several moments. He decides not to let this information change his good mood.

Nissim: Wait until you see what I got Ingrid, it's gorgeous. I know you haven't had the energy to shop so I bought presents for you to give out. They're wrapped so I'm going to have to tell you what's in everything.

Audrey: No more nuts?

Bruno enters with an old, red-painted, iron Christmas-tree stand, a box of small, colored, electrical bulbs, their wire and a small stepladder.

Bruno: Here. I can't find the ornaments. I don't even remember if there are any.

Nissim: Your parents must have had ornaments. If they gave you all this stuff they wouldn't keep the ornaments.

Bruno: Maybe they broke them, I don't know, leave me alone.

Nissim: I guess I could make some. String popcorn or something.

Audrey: We have popcorn?

Nissim: Audrey, it's time now for your nap.

Audrey: I'm not tired.

Bruno: No, Nissim's right, time for your nap, go on. Besides, Nissim and I need time to talk together, go on Audrey.

Nissim: I'll put an eggnog on your night table so when you wake up you can have it.

Audrey exits.

Bruno: The tree's very nice, Nissim, but think how much happier you'll be when you have your own tree in your own place. Won't that be great, a place of your own?

Nissim: This is my home.

Still talking, without thinking they put up the tree. Clearly they have performed many tasks together: one holds, the other one tightens the screws.

Bruno: Temporarily it is but not forever, you knew that when we moved in, we agreed to it, right?

Nissim: You said the apartment was temporary inasmuch as you one day wanted to buy a house when your career took off and you made a lot of money.

Bruno: But that house, if ever I purchased such a thing, would be for Audrey and myself, not you. We're a couple, Audrey and I. As a couple we'd be better off living alone, together. Do you understand?

Nissim: You mean without Ingrid?

Bruno: Yes, eventually, without Ingrid and without you.

Nissim: How about the baby? Would that be included?

Bruno: Nissim, listen to me, I think it would be best if you moved.

Nissim: I don't want to move.

Bruno: I know you don't but I think you should. I'd help you look for a new place, I'll help you paint it and fix it up, whatever.

Nissim has been testing the bulbs to see which light and which don't.

Nissim: The red ones are the only ones that work. They remind me of a street in Amsterdam where all these lonely people sat in windows with red lights on them.

Bruno: So what do you say, the day after New Year's we do a little apartment-hunting for you? Who knows, maybe we'll even find something in this building. Please be cooperative.

Nissim: I am cooperative, I know I am because I've been trying with every drop of my being. You're afraid I'll frighten the baby and be a neurotic influence upon it. Can't you see how hard I've been trying, how, out of sheer will power and hope for the future, I've cured myself of so many things — smoking, fainting, fits? I am not moving.

Bruno: Don't you miss your job? You could go back to it.

Nissim: Back to the sky? I was fired, I quit, there's nothing for me there anymore.

Bruno: Well what do you expect to do to earn money? You think you're just going to sit around here and be nanny?

Nissim: Maybe I'll get a job like yours selling things.

Bruno: They're not going to put someone like you in a commercial to advertise their product.

Nissim: Why not?

Bruno: Why not because Nissim you are from outer space and no one would ever drink the beer you chose or the cereal you poured in the morning.

Nissim: You just want to see me that way.

Bruno: What's to become of you, Nissim? Don't you ever give that any thought?

Harry Kondoleon

Nissim: If I stop thinking I can stop thinking you don't love me and think then that the baby will love me in the way no one and nothing has ever loved me.

Bruno: It's unnatural to put so much hope in one baby—what if it's retarded or deformed?

Nissim: Do you really think something like that would bother me? I'd love it any way it arrived.

Bruno: Go out and try to meet someone, will you try? Will you? No, you won't even make that small effort. Can't you wear clothes that are more flattering or at least fit? For example what the hell are you wearing? Is that supposed to be a maternity shirt or what?

Nissim: It's Vietnamese.

Bruno: What's to become of you? Ask yourself!

Nissim: It's true I don't spend every waking hour grooming myself and exercising and shopping for clothes. I guess I'm just a bad person! My teeth are good. They're straight at least. But they aren't the trouble, are they? The trouble is you don't love me.

Bruno: That's right! I don't! I don't love you in the way you mean, in the way you want me to.

Nissim: But you do love me.

Bruno: No I do not! We just covered that.

Nissim: You do, you just lack the self-knowledge to know it.

Bruno: Okay, Nissim, you want love, let's love. That's what you want, come on, let's love. Take off your things. There's lots of room on the floor, we can love right here.

Nissim *(Frightened)*: Stop it.

Bruno: Stop what? Love? Stop love? I love you, right? So let's do it, lover! Come on!

Bruno is assaulting Nissim.

Nissim: No, don't, please.

Bruno: No don't please what? No, you don't want love? No? It's all you talk about all day, have some! No? Then what kind of love are you talking about, Nissim, do you even know? You don't

90

love me, you just love someone who you know can't return it
so you have this protracted, stunted-adolescent crush!
Coward! Watching you watch me out of the corner of your eye
for the last ten years wondering if ever you'd find the courage
to make a move—just to get it over with once and for all and
out of the way! But you never did, did you? No, all your
energy is funneled into casting spells and deceiving yourself—
weakling! GET OUT OF MY LIFE!

*Enter Audrey holding a rubber baby doll wearing an absurdly
applied diaper.*

Audrey: Somebody put the diaper on the practice doll wrong.
Nissim *(From the floor)*: Why did Bruno become my friend at all,
Audrey, have you ever wondered? It's not a very difficult
question. Because I flattered him. Said things to make him feel
better, said them every day with loving regularity, said the
things I wished in my heart some voice, any voice, muttering
out of the darkness might say to me, bright comments and
boosters to face the day with and believe myself special—yes
I'm expert in these forms of speech—I just pretend he's me in
a happy dream and then I just say how good-looking he is,
how special, how smart and talented and apart from the
others. And when he modestly chimes in, "Oh no, I'm not," I
say, "Oh but you know you are." Who wouldn't like a friend
like that? Who doesn't need an excuse, any excuse, to believe
himself special and apart from the lump of humanity?
Bruno: All right, stop already.
Nissim: Stop what?
Bruno: Audrey, go back to bed.
Nissim: Audrey, reevaluate, because I think you should, your
choice of Bruno as the father of your baby. He doesn't love us.
He doesn't love anyone. He doesn't even love himself unless of
course the light is hitting him in some interesting way and he
happens to pass a mirror. When you get right down to it he'd
just as soon everyone drop dead. That way he could be left

alone with his mirror. Well, let him go there, to his friend the mirror. Friends, Audrey, are very fickle things, aren't they? One day they need you the next day they don't. Marian Free mentioned in passing they're killing the cologne commercial and that other thing is going off the air as well but said if anything came up she'd give him a call. Funny, I don't hear the phone ringing.

Bruno: Don't try to frighten me! I can get a job any day of the week if I wanted one, as if it were such a great thing to work!

Nissim: Think, Audrey, is this the man for your baby, a man who will twist it, seek only his own image in it and misapply the diaper?

Bruno: Look, I'm sorry.

Nissim: Sorry about what? That Christmas comes but once a year—we knew that already! I love you, it's a humiliating situation. I would love to not but I can't. Maybe I'll meet someone tomorrow in the lobby and forget about you but I doubt it.

Bruno: Audrey, tell him how his presence here is making it impossible for the two of us. You say you love me, well, I love her, can't you be sympathetic to that?

Nissim: Yes but I need things too! I don't really want to roll over and die as you might have me do. I need Audrey. I need Ingrid. I need their friendship. I always thought I needed you, I don't know why. And I need the baby, something to sink myself into.

Bruno: That's just it, you want to sink yourself into this blank infant—why not give it half a chance to develop into what it might.

Nissim: Why immediately assume I'll warp it? Why not believe I have something beautiful to tell it, games to play and lessons to teach? The baby will love me instantly, I know it as I know my name and you're jealous in advance knowing the baby will shrink from your touch, run screaming from you into my arms!

Bruno: See what I'm talking about, Audrey? With all the problems

in the world I'll be damned if one of the first things I'm going
to expose my only son or daughter to is a psychopath.

Nissim: So, I'm a weirdo, so what? Do you think if you repeat it
often enough I'll become ashamed and change?

Bruno: I never should have applied to that school. Better I should
have joined the army.

Nissim: You should have. You've never done anything for me
anyway except maybe make me feel more lonely and stupid.

Bruno: You're only attracted to jobs you aren't cut out for, to
people who can't love you, places you can't get to and
situations in which you don't fit in!

Nissim: Maybe you're right but then people like you are always
encouraging people like me to be weak with faulty loans of
strength.

*During this altercation the rubber doll has been pulled apart
by the two men.*

Bruno: What's wrong with you, Audrey—talk!

Nissim: She's sick of you that's what's wrong—I mean right—that's
right, we're all sick of you, Bruno.

Bruno: *SHUT UP!*

Nissim: Does Audrey know you've been fucking her mother?

*Pause. Nissim attaches the string of unplugged red lights to
the tree. Enter Ingrid with shopping bags filled with many
wrapped packages.*

Ingrid: It's four below zero thank God it's warm in here. You're
not going to believe what I bought, it's all too good.
Everything's wrapped but I don't think I'm going to be able to
wait until tomorrow, it's ridiculous to be so excited, I feel like
a little girl but then I haven't done anything for Christmas
since—well, I can't wait—this one's for you and Bruno,
Audrey—open it— *(Paying no attention to the lack of glee,
she excitedly opens the large wrapped package)* —look! Is

that corny: big wrapped box with envelope inside? Open the
envelope. *(She opens the envelope)* Tickets! Two tickets for
you and Bruno, Audrey. It's for a vacation, are you excited?
The whole idea is to fight postpartum depression and the best
way to do that is a holiday on the beach! I can take care of
the baby so there's nothing to worry about, hotel reservations
too. Right now you can't imagine wanting to leave the baby
that quickly after it's born but you will, believe me, and the
trip will seem a godsend. What happened to the practice
baby? *(She quickly sticks the head back on the body while
talking)* And this box here and I'm not going to open it is one
of the ones for the baby. Look at the elves on the wrapping
paper. Oh I can't resist opening it—is this evil? *(She rips open
the package)* Look! It's a hat! I'd sell my soul to have a head
this small to wear a hat so cute. *(She puts the hat on the doll)*
Don't you love it? And this one's for Nissim. *(She opens the
present without a second thought)* Look! You don't like it! Of
course you don't like it and why? Besides the fact it's
misshapen, a wretched color and the wrong size, it was sold to
me by a very, minus-the-goatee, handsome clerk, a clerk who
when I mentioned I needed to wrap two plane tickets said he
was very interested in air travel, said that he loved the
uniforms the pilots wear. I said I knew someone who had a
uniform very much like that—meaning you. The day after
Christmas you put on your uniform and return the pullover.
You go to his department with the credit slip in your hand and
you say you're interested in mysteries, he's a mystery-story
aficionado, you go to his apartment and a little this and a little
that and all mysteries are solved. Shave the goatee and he's
extremely handsome and I'm not just saying that—I mean not
handsome-handsome, but handsome, definitely good. Most of
these boxes are for the baby but this one's for me. *(She opens
it and laughs: it's a horse's head on a long stick, a toy for
children to ride. She rides it)* It's a riot isn't it! But I didn't
really buy it to ride. I bought it to copy. I thought I could do
a whole line of these things, not horses but the heads of

fantastical futuristic animals which is very popular now with children anyway—make them—use bright soft felts and feathers and these little nontoxic sequins—I bought a lot of the stuff already. Just in the elevator I thought of ten places that would carry them, toy and novelty stores, I'm positive I could sell the idea to a manufacturer and the originals of course I would give to the baby—why is everyone staring at me?

Bruno: Nissim told Audrey that you and I have been together.

Ingrid stops for a moment and then, angry, she slaps Nissim across the face.

Serves you right!

Ingrid: How could you tell her such a thing?!

Nissim: It's the truth.

Ingrid: The truth in this case distorts the truth. Did you think for a second what good could it do, that it could only upset her!

Nissim: What about me—I'm not upset? I'm upset to the marrow!

Ingrid: Audrey, it's nothing, less than nothing, a few ridiculous afternoons in which I felt a little less lonely and old. No one was trying to hurt or betray you I swear that—

Audrey: Am I named after a cat?

Bruno: What?

Audrey: Am I named after a cat?

Nissim: What cat?

Audrey: Aunt Rae told me you had a cat named Audrey and that you named me after it.

Bruno: This is a ridiculous conversation—

Audrey: Am I or am I not named after a cat?

Ingrid: So, I see, it's back to zero. Because of this insignificant little disclosure. The answer is yes. You are named after a cat, a cat I found.

Bruno: Audrey, you're getting yourself into a state over nothing, go back to bed.

Audrey: Your name's Elliot but you never mentioned that until Nissim said it.

Bruno: I never use that name, what difference does it make?

Audrey: That's right, none, no difference. My name's Audrey after a stray cat, but then the whole time growing up I never really knew my last name did I?

Ingrid: This again too? My last name, his last name, everybody's last name, does it change you, does it mean a thing?

Audrey: No, nothing means a thing. What ever made you think you'd make such a hot grandmother anyway? Who's to say you wouldn't get bored and walk away, leave it face down in the tub to run out and greet boyfriends?

Ingrid: And you, Audrey, what kind of mother will you make? You think you're purifying yourself by chopping us away. You might say I'm the last person in the world qualified to rate motherhood but to me, Audrey, you seem like a witch on an iceberg. Even when you make your sporadic efforts to "understand" I can always feel you backing off and judging, judging everyone. Is it worth it, waiting around for your forgiveness, I've often wondered!

Audrey: Maybe I'll just go away on my own, alone, away, what's to stop me?

Bruno: Away where?

Nissim: Take me with you.

Audrey: Chicago maybe.

Nissim: I could show you around I was born there.

Bruno: You were not!

Nissim: Just outside of Chicago.

Bruno: In Miami?

Audrey: Maybe I'll trip on a step in the snow and crush the baby before I even have it.

Nissim: No!

Audrey: Yesterday when I said I was taking the taxi to the doctor I didn't. I didn't go.

Bruno: You didn't go to your doctor?!

Audrey: I said I didn't. He handles me like a package that keeps returning. He's jealous of me, of my size.

Bruno: Audrey, are you going insane?

Audrey: I went to see my father. That's right, after all this time. I memorized the return address on the envelope you showed me and I went to visit him.

Ingrid: Good.

Nissim: How was it, meeting him?

Audrey *(Unaffected)*: Undramatic. He shook my hand, brought me a cup of milk and showed me stamps. He said his stamp collection is one of the largest in the United States and I had no reason to doubt him.

Bruno: I can't talk to you when you go into your dense-style.

Nissim: Isn't there a Spanish song called "Cuando Cuando Cuando"? Do you know? "Cuando Cuando Cuando."

Audrey: You thought you were revealing something to me telling those two have been at it. I knew that! Like attracts like. And I was never attracted to you, Bruno, not ever, I chose you the way I would a clock or typewriter, something that would efficiently give me something else and you have and here it is. The day I met you I threw my diaphragm onto the train tracks. Here, I said to myself, is a good breeder: good-looking, reasonably intelligent, quick, ambitious, steady-nerved, mature in the relative spectrum of the market and single. How could I be surprised if you revealed yourself base? I've never met a man I haven't found absurd and capable of any baseness.

Bruno: All right, go inside and lie down, you're just saying things randomly to hurt people and you don't mean any of them.

Audrey: I do mean them. I selected you, Bruno. Like a salmon. When you came into Marian Free's office I told myself, that's the one. I convinced her to take a second look at your resume. I convinced her—and it wasn't easy—to audition you again when you did so poorly.

Bruno: Only two things determine whether Marian Free will help you: one, if you call at the right moment, and two, whether or not you are good-looking—if you are she'll walk through fire for you—if you're not you won't get a glass of water.

Audrey: And you didn't call at the right moment.

Bruno: I'm going to measure my self-worth from a casting director? It's the kind of job only a child who was never invited to parties would want. Marian Free is a fool! She hasn't a shred of integrity. She's good at casting all right— casting people aside!

Audrey: She said you were vain and self-absorbed.

Bruno: And you're not? Confidentially, my dear, Marian Free was going to fire you. She said if you hadn't become pregnant and left she would have asked you to go. The best word she could come up with to describe you was *efficient*, otherwise clients complained constantly of your frosty demeanor and downright charmlessness so don't tell me about Marian Free! And on top of everything else she's a hedgehog.

Audrey: Was she such a hedgehog when you fucked her last June?

Bruno: Yes, as a matter of fact, she was. Did it bother you?

Audrey: No, nor did it the first four times she mentioned it in the office until on Friday I finally faked tears to satisfy her and shut her up.

Nissim: Marian Free?

Audrey: Don't look so shocked, Nissim, people who are one way all day are another way all night.

Nissim: I guess she's a fair-weather friend.

Bruno: She's an all-weather turncoat!

Nissim: I put contact paper on all the shelves in the kitchen.

Bruno: Who asked you to? No one wants it!

Nissim: Contact paper is hygienic.

Bruno: Contact paper is neurotic and Marian Free is a fool and a hedgehog!

Audrey: Pick on Nissim, that's handy having always someone around to spit at so you can feel less tiny.

Bruno: You told me you ran away from your mother and lived on your own after she threatened you with boiling water and stuck you with a fork.

Audrey: I made it up! I lied! You never saw a fork scar on my chest did you, Bruno? A child playing detective would have remarked on the absence but then you never did look much at my body while yours was there to choose from did you?

Bruno: Look, I'm sorry. Can we stop fighting? I'm sorry.

Audrey: Why? Because the cologne's a flop so all of a sudden everything smells shitty? There are other colognes, other shirts, ties, suits, robes, pajamas, cigarettes, vermouths and driver's seats to stick your face under or over or beside—or did you expect to merchandise yourself also as a father, or sell the baby itself, sell it up as an image, one more image for your pointless profligacy!

Bruno: I love you, Audrey, I do love you. I admit I've been shitty at showing it but I'll try harder, I'll be whatever you want me to be.

Audrey: And my mother? Do you love her too? What a fetching family circle we make: mother, mother, father and friend. And baby makes sideshow.

Bruno: I said I love you!

Ingrid: How can you love someone who's incapable of love? She's never loved anything. If I'm responsible for that so be it. I've tried, I've tried a hundred different ways of being a mother, a friend, a pal, a confidant, a nurse, even a maid. I've failed, you've failed, who cares! I want to move out of here. I wanted to be near the baby to find myself in it and renew my lease on life but I can't stand even another day here watching you isolate yourself further and further until I feel every gesture I make is some absurd call across a mob.

Nissim: We must believe in love, Audrey—human love—I do, I must, that's all there is on this planet and when there isn't any there's nothing.

Audrey: Love? *(She blurts out a garish laugh)* Love? What love? After some ten years of rubbing my body against others in the dark I'm here to say there is no love. Desire?—certainly. Tenderness?—occasionally. Empathy, kindness, momentary passions, okay, yes, maybe, but no love.

Nissim *(Punctured by arrows)*: No, no, Audrey, don't say that, please, it's so hard for me.

Audrey: Radio and television are mumbo-jumbo, newspapers and magazines are hieroglyphics, billboards and signs are obscenities, and the people in the street caterpillars crawling about afraid always of being squashed. You ask me have I cut myself off from life—*what life?* I'm born for the first time in here! I'm experiencing life from within me—the only place life can come from—I looked for it once in work, in friends, in sex, and found only shadows of those things, squat toneless shadows telling me one day was no different from the last. Do you know of any life out there? Go out and get it but don't bring it back to me!

Ingrid: No one can do enough for you, Audrey, can they?

Audrey: No, they can't.

Ingrid: Well then you are going to be a very lonely person, prepare yourself for that future now.

Audrey: You've already prepared me plenty, *Mother.*

Ingrid: With that attitude kill yourself now why don't you?

Audrey: I think of it sometimes, then I think, why bother? One expects everything to blow up in a minute anyway, suicide seems redundant.

Bruno: Audrey, I love you!

Audrey: Stop saying that to me—it's offensive. You think I'm ever going to let you fuck me again?

Bruno: Don't give me this I-fucked-you bullshit because the same time men are fucking women women are fucking men!

Audrey: May I quote you?

Bruno: And this sarcastic pingpong has got to go. It'll be bad for the baby.

Audrey: You are interested only in getting bigger, bigger in any shape or form possible, and mostly—and isn't this true, Bruno—it takes the form of sticking your penis anywhere you can inflate it. Don't ask me if I'm insane—you are jealous of me, you have been jealous for months as I've been getting larger and larger and you've been just some dumb balloon floating around the periphery of my event. You are all flat and flatness to me is hideousness. Look at me, I'm full, I'm filled now with all goodness and purity and I will not let it go, not for you not for the doctor not for anyone in this world.

She exits. Pause.

Bruno: What's with her?

Nissim: Her soul hurts.

Bruno: And what's this "soul" shit? That's the third time this week
    I've heard that expression around here—is everybody
    suddenly turning into Emily Dickinson or what? I told her I
    loved her what more does she want?

Nissim: I've felt the way she does, wanting amnesia, to wake up
    and forget everything.

Bruno: Amnesia? As it is you never know where you've put
    anything.

Nissim: Ingrid, did I tell you—

Bruno: Oh what didn't you tell us?! Have you let even one minute
    go by without one of your childhood recollections?

Nissim: Bruno, I'm trying to speak in a calm manner so as not to
    disturb you.

Bruno: Disturb me? I told you your very presence disturbs me!

Nissim: I'm sorry you feel that way.

Bruno: She called me a salmon! This is why she won't marry me—
    she hates me. She really hates me. Ingrid, say something, have
    you suddenly turned into a zombie—wake up and help me!
    I'm surrounded by fools and zombies! Somebody help me!
    Everyone's had a flip-out scene why not me, it's my turn—
    don't I get a mad scene?

Nissim: Have it.

Bruno: *"Have it."* I'd like to have it, with a chainsaw!

Nissim: Go ahead already.

*Bruno hollers, stamps his feet, punches the air, kicks the tree,
and storms out of the apartment.*

In fifth grade Laurie Ross and Cindy Brooks threw a party,
one of those parties where children pet and persecute each
other. They made a list of the invitees. Cindy's list fell out of
her looseleaf and I picked it up. Next to my name at the

bottom was a big question mark. When you have a big
question mark next to your name you never fully recover.
Wherever you go or whatever you do you have a question
mark, it's like having a tail.

Ingrid: Maybe we could bring a radio in here and play some
music.

Nissim: Songs on the radio fill me with such longing.

Ingrid: There might be a carol on, you'd like that.

Nissim: They remind me how I can't sing.

Ingrid *(Looking out the window between the slits in the Venetian
blinds)*: So many cabs outside, all rushing to some place. I
used to think a cab was something special, that I could just get
in one and it would take me away.

Nissim: I used to think that about airplanes.

Ingrid: I've run out of money.

Nissim: That doesn't matter, Ingrid! I'm going to support us now.
I'm going to be a model. Marian said she was going to keep
her eyes open for me.

Ingrid: What about this man in the store, why don't you arrange
to see him, maybe you could meet him.

Nissim: I couldn't. I'd be too afraid. I've never had the knack of
making friends, that's why I became an airline steward.

Ingrid: But you might fall in love and run away together.

Nissim: I couldn't! I can't! You don't understand. I was never a
teenager. I never went to beach parties and threw rocks into
the sea as if I'd live forever.

Ingrid: I don't remember my childhood. Hospitals and gravesites.
I rushed to have Audrey. I wasn't yet twenty. I wanted to be
related to someone alive.

Nissim: When I was little I went through a stage where I couldn't
go out if my shirt, shorts and socks didn't match. If my shirt
was maroon my socks had to have a maroon band around the
top and my shorts had to have maroon stripes or maroon in
the madras. I don't mean I was upset if these things didn't
match I mean I thought the top of the world would fly off and
not only myself but all people would be flung into ruin.

Ingrid: I'm going away.

Nissim: Wait, Ingrid, wait a little longer until the baby comes, then we could kidnap it and go away together!

Ingrid: I'm not going away alone.

Nissim: Not with Bruno.

Ingrid: No. *(Pause)* I met a man. A man in the subway. These plane tickets were for the two of us. I told him I wouldn't go but he insisted I take them hoping I'd change my mind and I have.

Nissim: It's a trick! If he's so rich he can run around handing out airline tickets what was he doing in the subway?

Ingrid: He says he likes it, the level of it. His mother just died and left him some money. He said he loved me.

Nissim: Oh, Ingrid, listen to yourself!—don't you see it's the same man—the man who left you!—all he did was change his face! He doesn't love you—the baby loves you.

Ingrid: That's the big fishhook isn't it, the baby. One wishes and wishes for so long for something, someone, to arrive and when it does it seems we're no longer fit for it anymore. Don't you see the way Audrey looks at me—and the baby if it looked at me that way I wouldn't be able to stand it—I would die! I'm leaving in the morning. I'll take an airplane to an island I've already forgotten the name of, I know it's hot there and the water around it will be like gin. I'll forget everything, I'll find some other shell, some otherwise ordinary seashell, pick it up and say this is my life now, this moment, this moment with no life before it and no life after it. It's a laugh isn't it, the new year. What new year? We never seem to be able to leave ourselves behind, do we. No matter what surgery we perform the bad limb seems to grow back eventually. Don't stare at me, it's enough that I'm admitting any of this out loud. Don't you think I'd like to rise up out of myself and be strong—who doesn't?! I've tried to alter my attentions but it's like a hex, life, the same spells return again and again, the only thing that changes is your face, every day you wake up and it's a little more haggard, a little more worn out, every day the lines of defeat drawn a little more thickly. Happy New Year.

Nissim: It's not Christmas yet.

Ingrid: Christmas, Halloween, the Fourth of July—does it make a difference?

Nissim: It has to! It has to or I can't wake up in the morning, can't bring my feet out from the covers, it has to matter, oh Ingrid, it can, we can make it matter! Oh, I know I sound like a baby but it's true, we can brighten our own days can't we? We don't have to wake up in a cloud depressed, desperate, angry, and waiting to die.

Ingrid: Make that philosophy work for you.

Nissim: I can't, not alone, I need to help someone, have someone help me.

Ingrid: You'll find someone like that.

Nissim: I won't—stay with me, Ingrid! If I've been getting on your nerves I'll change, I'll be quieter, I'll take up hobbies, I have the will power, I've proven it.

Ingrid: I'm going to my room to pack.

Nissim: You've lost faith—you can't lose faith! You haven't been reading the newspapers have you? I told you not to look at them, it's the same news over and over—they try to make you think it's some other news by making it more shocking on alternate days but it's the same thing and pieced together certainly to make us lose faith!

Ingrid exits.

DON'T ABANDON ME! (To himself, red alarm) I mustn't collapse. I must think of presents and happiness. *(He picks up the practice doll)* Oh little play-baby, do you love me? I love you. You do, I know you do. Why don't we open some of our presents, wouldn't that be fun? It's naughty but oh let's. What would be in this pretty box, hard to tell. *(He opens it, using occasionally the forced help of the practice doll)* A brush and comb set for you, how nice, but we'll have to put those away for a while until you're a little less bald. What could be in this big box? Let's just see. Ooo! A coat with matching little shoes.

Do you like them? Let's just try them on, okay? *(He puts the red baby coat and red shoes on the practice doll)* How dashing, how smart! You're a clever baby, ready for school already but I'll never send you to one of those public torture chambers don't worry or one of those schools named after saints that breed devils. I will teach you everything you need to know. Ask me a question. "Where do babies come from?" From God, little baby. "Who is God?" God is everything good and holy and pure and kind and healthy and growing and generous and good and good and good, that is God, little baby. "And where is he, where is God?" Why God is right above us, little baby, looking down on us. "Why then, tell me, why won't he help us, help us all, even just for a minute?" That's enough questions. We must get on our horse and ride away very fast from these questions, very fast because they will chase us, chase us through the day.

Practice doll in one arm, Nissim rides the horse toy, galloping speedily around the room. Enter Audrey.

Audrey: What are you doing?

Nissim stops short.

Nissim: I'm riding away with the baby.
Audrey: So am I. I called Aunt Rae and she's coming to pick me up.
Nissim: Ingrid met a man in the subway and said they were going to fly away together. Bruno left—he had a fit and slammed the door. *(Softly)* I didn't tell you, Audrey—I didn't want to frighten you, but you can't leave: I'd have nothing to live for, I'd have no dreams left. You'd be killing me, Audrey—that'd be on your conscience. I couldn't go on.
Audrey: I did a prayer, Nissim. I prayed for the first time since I was seven. I prayed for the happy answers. I waited and listened but the angels wouldn't talk.

105

Nissim: I have no place to go! My landlord tried to evict me, he said I was depreciating the building. I'd have to sleep on a cot in my aunts' hallway—Audrey save me!

Audrey: My suitcase is packed and on my bed, close it and bring it out here.

Nissim exits. Audrey sees a gift box under the tree marked for her. She opens the package. It is a diary. She flips through it reading a line here and there. Enter Ingrid.

Ingrid: I see you've opened your Christmas present.

Audrey: What is this?

Ingrid: A diary I started the day I left you. I always intended to give it to you. The first few months I wrote in it every day, then every few weeks, once a month, the whole thing trails off in the end.

Audrey: I don't really like to read.

Ingrid: I wanted you to know I was thinking of you.

Audrey throws the book down rather casually.

I tried to get you back, Audrey, I tried and tried. My sister— your aunt wouldn't let me near the house. All my letters came back unopened.

Audrey: A woman in the elevator said the Russians and the Americans have a new laser gun that can obliterate anything it points at.

Ingrid: I think how fast the last twenty years have gone by, how easily the next twenty could. If I live past that I'll be lucky to have someone push me in a wheelchair from one side of the room to the other. Better I should die and better now I should live even one year with someone who says they love me than suffer here like a dog.

Audrey: I used to wish you were dead because the idea of you being alive and having left me was so insulting it was unbearable. Consolation came in knowing you could never be happy:

wherever you'd go, whoever you'd be with, I would always be
there tugging at your conscience like a nail at a scab. I thought
even if I lived to be one hundred I would always be a deserted
seven-year-old screaming and kicking the walls until I grew numb
or was threatened I'd be stuck in an orphanage whichever came
first, I don't remember, I didn't keep a diary, there was nothing I
wanted to be reminded of or repeat to others.

Ingrid: You want to send me to hell, Audrey, save yourself the
trouble, I live there now.

Audrey: Clients would come into my office and flirt with me, very
attractive men, constantly. I loved rejecting them, rejecting
everything.

Ingrid: As I rejected you.

Audrey: That's right.

Ingrid: And nothing I can say or do will ever change that so why
talk about it. Nail the lid on it and bury it.

Audrey: I can't.

Ingrid: Walk on me if you think it would help but don't talk about
it anymore I can't stand it!

Audrey: It would I think.

Ingrid: What?

Audrey: Walk on you.

Ingrid: Literally?

Audrey: Yes. You walked on me at an age when walking on me
literally would have been more kind, so I'd be letting you off
easy if I walked on you.

Ingrid: And you'd forgive me, really forgive me if I consented, if I
let you walk on me?

Audrey: Yes, yes I believe I would.

Slowly, Ingrid lies face down on the floor.

Ingrid: All right, I'm ready. Step on me.

*Audrey steps up on her mother and walks back and forth all
over her with her pink slippers. Ingrid cries out occasionally*

with pain. The more Ingrid cries out the more satisfying it is to Audrey. Bruno enters with snow on his overcoat. Audrey does not notice him.

Audrey: Angels are whirling around me like rings—can you feel their light?! They're near me because I'm carrying one of their little sisters or brothers. I'm so afraid of letting it go because then day by day as the baby gets more and more like us the angels will ascend higher and higher until all I can see are the palms of their feet disappearing up into the ceiling.

Bruno takes off his ring and kneels at Audrey's feet.

Bruno: The world is a frightening place, Audrey, and things of course could be better. They could be better for everyone but that doesn't mean we have to live like leftovers on a sinking ship. I could be a better man and I'll try to be, I swear it. I'm sorry it's offensive to you when I say I love you. I do love you, Audrey, and I'll work to make that expression mean something for the first time if it's never meant anything before. Please marry me. Say yes, take it and say yes.

Ingrid *(Underfoot)***:** Say yes, Audrey.

Enter Nissim with Audrey's suitcase.

Nissim: Why are you wearing your coat indoors?

Bruno: Don't ask me why I'm on one knee or why Audrey's standing on her mother.

Nissim: You're proposing marriage and she's making up with her mother.

Bruno: Say yes, Audrey, marry me. Take my ring.

Nissim: Say yes, Audrey, marry him. Take the ring. Take it. My parents stayed happily married until they knifed each other. Take the ring. Everyone take what they have to and go.

Bruno: I'll never leave you, Audrey.

Audrey: Yes. Yes.

Bruno slips the ring on Audrey's finger, she steps off her mother and has a painful contraction.

Bruno: Audrey is that your first?

Audrey: They started this morning.

Bruno: What! Oh my God where's your suitcase?! *(He sees it and grabs it)* Thank God your aunt's pacing in the lobby—she can drive us to the hospital.

Audrey: I'm having it, oh God, I'm having it. I'm ready, Nissim, I'm ready, Mommy, Bruno, I'm ready, I'm having it, I'm ready, I'm ready.

Bruno picks up Audrey and with some difficulty carries her, her legs somewhat astride, and the suitcase out of the apartment. Nissim looks out the window through the Venetian blinds. Ingrid doesn't move from the floor. After some moments Nissim lifts the blinds, it is gently snowing.

Nissim: It's snowing. Everyone looks so sad and lost in the snow. Suddenly I'm so tired. Here's your present, Ingrid. I'll open it for you. *(He opens it, inside the box there is a beautiful blue silk scarf. He kneels to show it to her)* It goes in a way with the blouse you wore the day I met you. I left the price tag on it in case you hated it.

Ingrid: You shouldn't have spent so much.

Nissim: That's the store code, this is the price. *(He plugs in the tree. The red lights go on and off, on and off)* The cradle looks so alluring, doesn't it? Do you think it would break if I got in it? I'm getting in. *(He climbs into the cradle. After a moment, in the cradle, face up, pitiless)* I listen to records at the wrong speed and don't know it. I put quarters in other people's machines at the laundromat and watch the clothes spin and dry while mine sit in a wet unattended lump. I'm a tragic character and the tragedy of it is I have to go on living. If only I knew there was some curtain to be drawn or light that could go out and I could go home and be someone else it would be bearable but I have no place to go and no one else to be.

Ingrid has picked up her diary, she opens it and reads from it.

Ingrid: Dear Audrey, today I went to the beach and burned my skin. I can't sleep. Yesterday was your birthday and I bought you a flower in the street. I can't concentrate for the clatter of the petals falling on the nighttable near the clock and the breath of the man I love hot on my neck, the sound makes me shiver and I feel as old as the world and I want to call out has anyone ever been so alone? Tomorrow and tomorrow. I want to read this one day and laugh.

She rips out the page, laughs, and weeps, covering her face with the blue scarf. The snow falls. The red tree lights blink. The cradle rocks back and forth. Curtain.

THE END

The
Vampires

CHARACTERS

Cc, 35.
Ian, 37, Cc's husband.
Ed, 33, Ian's brother.
Pat, 33, Ed's wife.
Zivia, 13, Pat and Ed's daughter.
Porter, 30.

TIME

June, the present.

SETTING

Cc and Ian's home, the living room. This is a very old, facelifted, Victorian house. No expense has been spared to recoup the Victorian detail to excellent condition. What is amazing about this room—and it is amazing, as well as being starkly beautiful—is the contrast between the room and the objects in it. The furniture, except for a classic, wine red, Victorian couch, is ultramodern. There aren't many paintings and sculptures but those that are present are up-to-the-second contemporary. There is a very large window on the upstage wall framing a drooping tree outside. Although the room seems a design hybrid of the city, we are in the country.

N O T E

The song "I Put a Spell on You" by Screamin' Jay Hawkins
appears at designated points throughout the script as well as being
played in its entirety near the end of the play. The words to this
song are:

I put a spell on you
Because you're mine
Stop the things you do
Watch out
I ain't lying
Yeah
I can't stand no running around
I can't stand no putting me down
I put a spell on you
Because you're mine
Oh yeah

Stop the things you do
Watch out
I ain't lying
I love you
I love you
I love you anyhow
I don't care if you don't want me I'm yours right now
I put a spell on you
Because you're mine
Mine
Mine
Oh you're mine.

ACT ONE

*Late at night. The room is dark. Cc and Ian enter. Cc turns
on a light switch. She is wearing a strapless black evening
dress and a small black cocktail hat with a thin black feather
pointing downward. He wears a tuxedo, bow tie undone. Ian
is avoiding Cc, nervously going about the room, fixing himself
a drink, grumbling to himself.*

Cc: I'm unhappy, I can't live this way, the way you are. Don't run
away from me, Ian. We have problems, we should sit down
and work them out. Don't ignore me, Ian. A drink isn't going
to help—I know. Listen to me! Do you not love me anymore,
Ian? Is that it? Say so then, that you don't need me or want
me. Maybe we need a separation. If we need one let's have one
then but tell me. Tell me we should have one. Talk to me!
Where are you going—you're not going to bed!

Ian exits upstairs.

Get back here! You have got to show me some consideration.
Do you hear me? I thought you wanted to go to this ceremony.
I didn't want to go. I thought it meant something to you. I
broke my neck trying to finish this dress for tonight. You
make fun of it in front of the first group of people we meet—
how am I supposed to interpret something like that, Ian? Am I
supposed to take it as a joke? How can I? Come down here!
Oh who am I kidding with this dress anyway?! *(While speaking*

*she painstakingly removes the bottom part of the dress which
has been pinned on. The seam isn't even sewn so, unpinned, it
is a large, black, stiff piece of fabric. She is left with the top
of the dress, panties, dark stockings and high-heeled shoes)*
The invitation says black tie and half the people show up in
dungarees and pullovers so I look like a Mardi Gras float and
then the editor of that coarse magazine you used to work for
points out the pins in my dress as if she were uncovering a sex
scandal! Ian! Ian! Are you coming down here? I'm trying to be
understanding, Ian. I know you're going through a difficult
career-transition period. Maybe some of your behavior these
last few weeks has something to do with that actor's tragedy.
That's not your fault, Ian, many actors get bad reviews, they
just have to live with it, no one's to blame, you were just doing
your job. But when you started laughing tonight during that
woman's acceptance speech I was never so embarrassed in my
entire life and you being one of the judges! But then I've lost
count of most of the humiliations: you mimicking people at
checkout counters, alienating each and every person we meet,
contradicting me in front of my friends. I know I have very
idealistic ideas about love but this marriage, Ian, is hitting
some uncharted new low.

*Ian has raced down the stairs and, surprising her from
behind, grabbed Cc and set his mouth at her neck.*

Oh you think we're just going to kiss and make up?

*She feels his teeth in her neck and screams. Blood-sucked, she
collapses faint onto the couch, half-sitting, half-slumped over.
Ian exits scurrying away back upstairs, wiping his mouth
with his sleeve on the way out. After a moment, a young girl,
Zivia, opens the window, climbs into the room, taking no
notice of Cc, who isn't entirely visible to her on the couch.
Zivia inserts a tape cassette from her pocket into the stereo*

*component. Screamin' Jay Hawkins sings "I put a spell on
you/ Because you're mine." Zivia, expressionless, dances
oddly in place. The sun rises. Cc does not stir. There's a
knock at the door followed by more knocking and a woman,
Pat, calling.*

Pat *(Offstage)*: C. C. Are you up? It's me, Pat. C!

*Zivia hears the knocking, quickly removes her cassette and
runs into the kitchen. Pat opens the unlocked door and
hesitantly enters. She is a small, brown-haired woman dressed
very casually in jeans.*

C, are you awake? It's me, Pat. Are you up?

Cc's eyes half open, dazed. Pat is agitated.

I know I should have called. I'm so worried and upset I
couldn't sleep so I got in the car and just drove. Is Zivia here
with you? You can tell me, C. There's no use hiding it. I won't
be jealous. I know you two are very close and Zivia's very fond
of you and all so I wouldn't be surprised. In fact, you're the
first person I thought of. I thought, Zivia's gone to visit her
Aunt C, that's all. Is she here? No? C, you know I can't take
this, this kind of extreme worry. I mean since Axel four years
ago my nerves have been shot to hell. So I can't be accused of
jumping to conclusions when Zivia doesn't come home Friday
and all day Saturday! I mean, what is going on?! I'm not an
overprotective mother, far from it. Perhaps I should be.
Maybe that's where I've gone wrong but you don't have any
children, C, so you can't sit there and accuse me! I mean it's
one thing to go off on a day of shopping with a niece and quite
another to raise a daughter all year every year worrying what's
going to happen to her. So don't accuse me of anything! Do
you know that two girls in Zivia's class took their own lives—

two! In my class there were none. Maybe it's nowadays the rage but, frankly, I'm terrified! You know what kind of touchy type Zivia is and you know my pop took a shot at himself. I mean that kind of thing is maybe hereditary. I don't know. I just don't want to set anything off and you know what Ed's like. He found some pot or something in her room and started yelling and cursing at the top of his lungs. I mean pot's no big deal, C. All the kids smoke pot. I smoked pot. Big deal, I said, Ed, calm down! Does my hair look funny? It didn't curl the way they said it would on the box. So she's not here?

Cc: Pat.

Pat: What's wrong with you? Are you drunk? What are you wearing?

Cc: Pat, I think Ian bit me.

Pat: Bit you? Ian? Where?

Cc: On my neck.

Pat: He bit your neck? *(She looks)* You do have a little mark. You sure it's not a lovemaking thing?

Cc: I didn't actually see him. He attacked me from behind. We were having a fight, sort of, actually, I was. Ian's gotten very difficult lately but it's just a phase. He passes through these things. Maybe it was someone else.

Pat: Do you always keep your door open?

Cc: It's usually locked. Help me to the mirror. Look at it, oh my God, it's savage.

Pat: It's just a little thing. Are you sure it's not a hickey?

Cc: Hickeys don't leave two holes in your neck.

Pat: Well, they might as well. You know, Cc, I shouldn't even be here, Ed's so mad at Ian. He said he was going to kill Ian.

Cc: That review was too harsh, I told Ian that.

Pat: Too harsh? C, he took a shit on Ed's play. His own brother! And he had no business reviewing it in the first place. It was a workshop thing with an invited audience. My teller's son who's in the theater said that's not done, just not done!

Cc: Pat, if you recall, Ed asked Ian to do a piece on the play.

Pat: Yes, a promotional thing to work up some interest in it, not squelch any little there was!

Cc: I don't know what to say, Pat. I have no control over what Ian writes. If it's any consolation to you and Ed, the paper let go of Ian.

Pat: What about that magazine?

Cc: That was freelance and they've more or less put a freeze on him too. It seems there was some unfortunate circumstance with some actor Ian dealt rather severely with who jumped out of a hotel window. The actor's family, it turns out, was very well connected with the paper and, well, I really don't know any of the details but Ian says he's through with journalism.

Pat: But he can go back if he wanted to, can't he? I mean if he changes his mind and all. Newspaper people forget everything from one day to the next. They'd hire him back, wouldn't they? Ed's like that, once a month it's, I'm through with cabinets! I've made my last cabinet!

Cc: I hope you'll take this in the right vein, Pat, but you know as well as I do Ed's not really a writer. It's just something he felt like dabbling in, like a hobby or an experiment so he can't really take Ian's review to heart. I agree with you that it was very cruel but Ed can't let it eat at him, not something so inconsequential really when you think of it. Ed's a very successful carpenter; that's what he is and that's good for him.

Pat: I know you're going to find this hard to believe, C, but a lot of people thought a lot of Ed's play. No—I'm not talking about Ed's barber and the paperboy. I mean people of influence, influential people, people who read and write books.

Cc: Well, great, have some of those people help Ed do—

Pat: No! Ian's review made everyone lose faith! Nothing is possible without good publicity! Why do you think that actor jumped out of his window?

Cc: But, Pat, it's done already—what do you want Ian to do?

Pat: A retraction! Have him write a complete retraction.

Cc: That's not possible, have you ever seen such a thing?

Pat: People do it all the time. You want the two brothers together again, don't you? You say Ian's out of work, in a bad mood, going through hard times—he's going to need Ed's help.

Cc: What do you mean?

Pat: You were an only child, C. You don't understand family politics the way I do.

Cc: I do think they should be reconciled. Maybe that's all this is with Ian, just a mood thing. He's always been a moody man, that combined with perhaps guilt over that actor's death. But, Pat, do you really think that—

Ed knocks at the door.

Pat: Oh my God, I hope that's not Ed!

Ed opens the door and enters. He is a bit larger than his brother.

Ed! What are you doing here?

Ed: Hello, C.

Cc: Hi, Ed.

Pat: Ed, your brother bit your sister-in-law.

Cc: It's true, Ed, Ian bit me, I think.

Ed: Well, I'm not surprised!

Cc: I'm sorry about the review. I really am, honestly.

Ed: Sure, sure, we're all torn up about it.

Pat: Cc's agreed to get Ian to write a retraction.

Cc: Pat, I don't know if I can. I said I'd try, I—

Ed: I don't want a retraction. You think I came here for a retraction? I came here to get my wife and daughter.

Pat: Ed, Ziv's not here.

Ed: Yes she is.

Cc: She's not, Ed.

Ed: Her friend's father called—

Pat: Michelle called?

Ed: Her father. And he said the two of them have been calling each other back and forth all night and when he listened on the receiver he heard—

Pat: Well, C, to harbor my own daughter from her own mother and seek to deceive me—!

Cc: I swear to you she's not here!

Ed: She is but only momentarily because when I get my hands on her she's going right home and from there reform school.

Zivia springs out of the kitchen. She has tangled hair. She's thin with a dark, expressionless face. She is not dressed in the trendy accoutrements of the moment but rather some mix-and-match deal she has construed which is peculiarly her own.

Zivia: I'm not going home!

Cc: Zivia!

Ed: Get in the car.

Pat: Let me handle this. Zivia, listen to your father and get in the car.

Zivia: I'm not going home and I'm not getting in the car.

Ed: Oh no? Where are you going?

Cc: Zivia, how long have you been here? Where have you been sleeping? You know you could have come directly to me. If you have a problem maybe I can help you.

Pat: I think you have enough problems of your own, C. Get in the car, Zivia, before your father loses his temper.

Ed: I'm not losing my temper—don't bait me, Pat. Tell me, Zivia, because I'm a curious guy, if you're not going in the car and you're not going home, where are you going?

Zivia: *Cross* country.

Pat: Cross-country?!

Ed: No. That's very interesting. Cross-country. Now where, pardon me please for my nosiness, where do you expect to get the money to go cross-country? Don't tell me!—from the same place you get money for everything else, from stealing from your parents. Well, that may have been all well and good to

buy books and ridiculous clothing—that being more fun I
suppose than asking directly for it—as if your parents might
deny you anything, Zivia—have we ever, Zivia?!

Pat: Ed.

Ed: No, it must be more fun to go through our wallets—as if we're
too stupid, Zivia, to see when I put two hundred dollars in my
wallet and you leave two! You think I'm not going to notice!
You think I'm one of your stupid friends from school?!

Pat: Ed.

Cc: Ed, I'm sure there's an explanation. You needed to borrow the
money for something maybe, Ziv, for a friend in trouble?

Ed: Oh there's an explanation for everything, for everything in the
world, I know that! But I want to hear it in Zivia's own words.
What are you doing with this money, Zivia?

Pat: Can't we do this at home, Ed?

Ed: In your own words, Zivia, tell your aunt what you do with
money you steal from your parents.

Zivia: I don't steal.

Ed: I'll beat you, Zivia, so help me God, I'll beat the shit out of
you right here and now!

Cc: Ed, let me talk to Zivia in the kitchen alone for five minutes,
all right? All right, Pat? Just for five minutes.

Ed: Okay, Zivia, for the sake of argument we'll pass on the
stealing and I'll rephrase my question. Here it comes and
listen closely because this is your last chance. What, Zivia,
with chunks of money that mysteriously come your way, do
you purchase? In your own words.

Zivia: Records.

Pat: Records are expensive.

Ed: You know what I happened to bring with me today, Zivia—
your record collection! *(He dumps drugs and drug
paraphernalia out of his pockets)*

Zivia: I was guarding it for a friend.

*Ed runs after Zivia, who tries to dodge him. He catches her
by the hair and hits her.*

Ed: What friend? Michelle? You're a fucking little liar my dear girl and you're going to an all-girl prison before I let any of this shit continue. How stupid can you be, Zivia? No one uses this shit anymore, only morons and scuzz. I told you six hundred times, didn't I, my best buddy in school they found him with a needle in his arm dead. You want them to find you that way, Ziv, a stiff?!

Pat: Ed, let go of her hair already!

Zivia: Aunt Cc, remember I told you about my friend Benta Strong who played piano all day and people said she could be a prodigy and play professionally? On the last day of school she left a note on a string around her neck that said goodbye and then—

Pat *(Panicked)*: I forbid you to speak of that girl! Ed—you see what you did? Zivia, if you say these things are Michelle's we'll believe you but we'll have to forbid you from storing them for her.

Ed: Don't be a jackass, Pat. She's laughing at us with this suicide shit. You want to kill yourself, honey, just keep fucking with this shit and you'll be playing duets soon enough with your little friend and you won't even have time to write a goodbye.

Cc: Ed, sit down and have a cup of coffee with Pat and let me have five minutes in the kitchen with Zivia. We'll just have a little talk and report back to you two, is that all right? Come, Zivia, just you and me and I'll make us some toast with Four Fruit Jam you like, okay? Go in the kitchen, Ziv.

Zivia exits.

Ed, Pat, sit down, I'll bring two cups of coffee right out.

Ed and Pat sit. Cc exits.

Ed: Ian bit her?

Pat *(Half-shrugging)*: That's what she said.

Cc enters with two cups of coffee.

Cc: Just how you like it, Ed, two sugars, and Pat, black. Just give us a few minutes and you just relax. *(She exits)*

Pat: What route did you take?

Ed: Never mind what route I took, I'm here.

Pat: I'm just asking because I didn't see your car. Which car did you take?

Ed: What do you mean what car did I take? You took one, didn't you? Well, I took the other one! Are you turning into a dope, Pat, or what?

Pat: Okay, there's no point in picking on each other. Wouldn't you be satisfied if Ian wrote a retraction?

Ed: No, I wouldn't be satisfied, it's not enough. I want more.

Pat: Sometimes you can want a lot and get nothing.

Ed: Keep your philosophy to yourself. You've done enough harm with Zivia as it is.

Pat: Me?!

Ed: Who else? Who indulges and spoils her, small wonder she's wayward.

Pat: Who buys her anything she points at and—

Ed: What about the things you point at, Pat, you don't get those?

Pat: I have my own salary.

Ed: Don't make me laugh!

Pat: Okay, if she kills herself it'll be your fault, not mine.

Ed: Why do you keep bringing that up? She knows it's your alarm button and she presses it every time she needs you as an ally!

Pat: How do you expect me to behave? You haven't completely forgotten about my pop have you?

Ed: Your pop, your pop—I already told you those things are not inherited, Pat.

Pat: How do you know? Children give out messages, you have to be able to read them. Just the other day Zivia showed me this story in a book about a girl who ran away from home and never came back.

Ed: And that you took as a message?

Pat: She ran away, didn't she? I wouldn't be so smug if I were you,
Ed. Part of the reason Zivia took up with these new friends is
because year after year you've insisted on putting up that
light-up Nativity that has alienated all but the lowliest in our
neighborhood!

Ed: What are you saying? Are you drunk?

Pat: Mr. Platz, Mr. and Mrs. Maguire, Mr. and Mrs. Little—I still
have some of those polite notes—"Please-don't-light-that-thing-
up!"

Ed: And this is your theory on why our daughter is taking drugs?

Pat: I don't know that she is taking drugs! I haven't seen her take
any, have you? She says she doesn't. I know that if you bought
her that Beta-Max the way she wanted and the way I told you
to, she wouldn't be spending all her time at Michelle's who has
one. Michelle's father has tapes of old TV shows and they
watch them and I wouldn't be surprised if they smoke pot
while they watch those shows. So what. I smoked pot when I
was a teenager and so did you.

Ed: Pat, have you looked at this stuff? We're not talking about
pot. And just for the record, I tried pot and did not like it. It
made me slow and lethargic like the rest of the world and that
I did not like and consequently I did not use pot!

Pat: All right, stop yelling!

Ed: You've got this blind spot with Zivia, can't you see that? And
it's because of Axel, your guilt over Axel.

Pat: I have forbidden you to speak on that subject. Subject
closed.

Ed: Your guilt over Axel, but get over it, Pat. We are innocent: I'm
innocent and you're innocent. Or do you want every year of
your life to feel like the one before it, never moving forward,
never getting anywhere, forever harping on the grim unhappy
accidents that happen in life? You close the subject, not me!
I'm getting my play on—that I can promise you—and that shit
of a brother is going to help me if I have to cut off his right
arm and use it myself—retraction my ass!

Pat *(Mimicking Cc)*: "Ed's a very successful cabinetmaker, that's what he is and that's good for him," that's what she says. I got their number when they didn't show up at our wedding.

Ed: They're the kind of people my play attacks, no wonder they don't like it, two phonies!

Pat: You said it!

Ed: Most so-called art is total bullshit and everybody knows it and nobody needs anyone to tell them so! My play isn't art and I don't want it to be because it's real; it's talking to real people about real things and it's only the phonies, who are *unreal*, who can't see that, can't see what kind of thing I have written: *American*, an *American* play, a play about the colonists, the Indians, the revolution, the whole scene! All that projected and juxtaposed—whatever—upon or with today's problems— unemployment, taxes, crime, taxes, demoralization of the people, racial tensions, joblessness, freeloaders, taxes, defense, taxes—you're going to tell me this is a play that's not going to be a commercial success?!—something that reaches out and communicates to people on their own level, people who want to see this country on the right road again if ever there was a right road and little fuckoffs like my big brother would have it otherwise. But take it from me—every dog has his day!

The upstairs door slams and Ian, still in his disheveled tuxedo, comes down the stairs and enters the room. He throws down on the couch his pillow and folded pajamas.

Pat: Hello, Ian.

Ian ignores Pat and Ed and, seeing the bright shining light from the window, grunts and shuts the shade and curtain.

Ed: Don't you have anything to say to me, Ian?

Ian: Yes: you bore me.

126

Ian titters at his own joke. The room is suddenly rather dark,
lit from one small green lamp.

Pat: Why are you getting rid of all the light?

Ian *(Matter-of-fact)*: Because I hate it, hate the light, all light things,
the sun, the day, grass, flowers and you two standing there. I hate
everything. I've decided to become indiscriminate.

Pat: Ian, did you bite Cc because Cc says you did.

Ian: Yes, as a matter of fact, I did.

Ed: I wasn't surprised.

Ian: No, no, you wouldn't be. Pat, can you guess what I've
become? Guess.

Pat: A dog?

Ian: Something better.

Ed: A rat?

Ian: A vampire. I have, really. I don't mean it as a form of speech.
I bit Cc and sucked her blood. I tasted it and liked it, liked
having it in my mouth to slosh around. And I want more. I've
become evil. *(He laughs)*

Pat: Evil?

Ian *(He finds the bottom of Cc's dress, flaps it over his shoulders,
ties it around his neck, creating a makeshift cape)*: E-V-I-L,
heard of it? Look!

Ed: I have an idea, Ian.

Ian: Hmm?

Ed: My idea is that you stage another reading of my play here in
your house and you invite influential people to see it and you
be in it.

Ian: I have another idea. Why don't I bite Pat?

Pat: Keep away from me, Buster. I'm the one who defended you
when Ed read that trash-job you did and was going to come
over here and cut off your balls with a machete!

Ed: Listen, Ian, you ruined my chances to get attention for a play
I worked very hard on, a play that meant a lot to me and still
does.

Ian: You had no business writing it. Your business is nailing wood together.

Ed: That's not for you to say!

Ian: Then why did you invite me to the silly reading, Ed? I didn't want to go. Why did you take me aside and ask me to write something on it? I told you I didn't want to. You said it was the biggest favor you would ever ask of me. Isn't that the way it went?

Ed: Certainly you didn't think I wanted you to slaughter it!

Ian: It was a mercy killing, Ed. Save what's left of your face and burn the surviving copies.

Ed: That play talks for people who wouldn't ordinarily get a voice in the theater!

Ian: True, and there must be no inducement for them to open what is far better left shut.

Ed: You hate that play because it's patriotic, that's why you hate it.

Ian *(Plain)*: Your play is idiotic, Ed. It makes no sense. It's incoherent, it's naive, it's stupid. Do you understand?

Ed: Haven't you found out, Ian, that all your cute epigrams make a lot less sense in practice than in theory—that although they sound amusing they're just not true?

Ian: No, actually I haven't found that out at all. I don't suppose I ever will.

Ed: Well, you should.

Pat: Those are your best put-downs, Ian? We hear better on TV.

Ian: I don't doubt it, you two being in the forefront of its most unwavering fans. I'm surprised you're here at all, breaking the vigil.

Pat: Pseudointellectual!

Ian: Oh! That hurt!

Pat: You're losing your hair, Ian.

Ian: Don't you think I know that?

Pat: You're going to need a wig, Ian.

Ed: Okay, Pat, let me handle this.

Pat: I know why he's acting this way—Cc told me. Because that actor jumped out of his window so now you feel rotten and you're biting everyone to feel better!

Ian: You think I was upset when that actor jumped out of his window? I laughed! My only hope was that more of the hambones in that whorish profession would take his cue!

Pat: You're going to hell.

Ian: I want to go to hell. I'm praying for it, really, I have. I've drawn pornographic pictures with a red marker in my Bible but I'm still here so I guess that doesn't work. I've thought unclean thoughts, touched myself and bit my wife and yet no hell. You went to Catholic school, Pat, suggest something to me so I can go to hell.

Ed: Are you trying to be a comedian, Ian?

Ian: Not me!

Pat: Ed, have him write the retraction.

Ed: I'm handling this. Ian, I'm making you a proposition plain and simple. I'm willing to forgive you for ruining my play with your review if you agree to put the play on and—

Ian *(Yawning very loudly)*: I'm so tired! Now that I'm a vampire I'll be sleeping days and waking nights.

Ed: You say you've become a vampire, Ian. Maybe we'll just stick a stake through your heart and bury you in the backyard.

Ian: Oh, I don't know how I'd like that.

Ed: No? No, I don't suppose you would. How about if I just beat the shit out of you?

Ed grabs Ian and punches him several times very hard and swiftly. Ian collapses to the floor with a bloodied face.

Pat: Don't kill him!

Ed: Little prick with this monster-movie bullshit! Says he's a vampire! Of course he's a vampire—he's never been anything else but one except maybe a sponge or a scumbag! Just another attention-getting device!

Pat: Stop yelling.

Ed: Not unlike his fake colds, fake headaches, fake hives, fake depressions and fake nervous breakdowns. The whole time growing up it was dealing with Ian's frustrations—mad because he was puny and argumentative so no one ever wanted him on their team. Maybe the college I went to wasn't as good as the one he went to but I was the *star* of my college, everyone knew my name—when I'd walk out of my frat house everyone would go, "Hi Ed!"

Ian *(Woozily waving)*: Hi, Ed.

Holding Ian up by the shirt, Ed goes to punch him again and Ian holds up his hand in truce.

Wait! Wait. Maybe it is possible there's something we could salvage from the script.

Pat: Oh now it's wait wait, two seconds ago you were ready to bite us. Your teeth aren't as sharp as you thought they were are they, Ian?

Ed: Shut up, Pat, I'm handling this. *(He helps Ian to his feet)* So you think the script has possibilities.

Ian: Yes, possibilities.

Ed: And you'll do it?

Ian: Well, I have to give this some thought. The script, of course, could use some work.

Ed: I admit it needs a little touching up.

Ian: Perhaps something could be spun from the thread of it but it would take certain cuts and changes and weaving here and there. You'd have to trust me completely to do what's best for it.

Pat: And be in it.

Ian: Oh, I'd be in it.

Ed: That's great, Ian, we can all be in it! There's five parts with the Indian. We can each have a part and Zivia could be the Indian!

Pat *(Skeptical)*: And we could put it on here, Ian? And you'll invite the VIPs to come see it?

Ian: Yes, I will. Now that I think of it I think that would be a topnotch idea. I can really picture it, your play, Ed, performed by us, Zivia as the Indian, and all the VIPs, as you put it, Pat, seated here around the room clapping and cheering us on.

Ed: It'll be great! I can't wait! How soon can you get them all here?

Ian: Well, that's hard to say and then of course there's the work I have to do yet on the script.

Ed: A week?

Ian: Let's say about a week.

Ed: A week. And you'll invite the people?

Ian: Oh, I'll invite them all right.

Pat: And they'll come?

Ian: Oh, they'll come.

Ed: Gosh, Ian, I'll never ask another favor of you, never. I'm so happy. Pat, I have the tent in the trunk, we can hitch it up outside.

Pat: The tent?

Ed: Yeah, so we can camp out the week until the presentation.

Ian: Camp out?

Pat: Ed.

Ed: Yeah, Pat and I don't want to infringe on you and Cc and we're used to camping out.

Ian: Right.

Pat: Ed.

Ed: We'll just come in to use the facilities and this way I'll be handy if you want to ask me questions about something.

Ian: Well, everything's all set, I think I'll go downstairs to bed. Tell C I'm sleeping in the cellar now.

Ed: Okay.

Ian: And have her ring up the butcher. I want a pitcher of blood when I wake up.

Ed: Sure thing. Wait—don't you want the script so you can work on it? *(He takes the rolled-up script out of his back pocket and hands it to Ian)* Now, don't hesitate to come up if you have any problems—

Ian: Okay, don't worry, bye. *(He exits through a door to the basement)*

Pat: You see, you two can get along if you make an effort.

Ed: Are you kidding?—I know that! In a lot of ways we're very much alike.

Pat: Did you see how he was licking his own blood after you punched him? Do you think he's really what he said he was, a vampire?

Ed *(Condescending)*: He means it figuratively.

Pat: But he said he likes to drink blood.

Ed: What's wrong with you, Pat? Even when things are going well you've got to look for something negative to pick at.

Pat: I can live without your nasty comments, Ed, and all those little I'll-handle-its—who do you think you're talking to?

Ed: Everything's going well, that's all I'm saying.

Pat: Is he writing a retraction?

Ed: This is better than the retraction!

Pat: I don't know. Can't you get trichinosis from blood?

Cc enters, costume unchanged.

Cc: Pat, Ed, I think you should sit down. It's not a light matter. To be quite frank, I think we have what could be a serious problem on our hands.

Ed: What problem? What are you talking about?

Cc: Zivia, Ed.

Ed: We already know she's taking drugs, what problem could be worse?

Pat: We don't know for a fact she takes drugs, Ed. Let's not jump to conclusions.

Cc: She doesn't admit to taking them but I'm sure she is. But that's not the real problem.

Ed: Not the real problem!

Pat: Ed, calm down.

Cc: The problem is she's thirteen years old and she's a virgin and she doesn't have a boyfriend so of course she feels like the last one on earth—I mean I know these problems seem like nothing to you and me but to her they're devastating.

Ed: Do you mean to stand there and tell me a thirteen-year-old girl should be anything *but* a virgin? Are you out of your fucking mind?!

Cc: I'm not saying she shouldn't be one. I'm saying she's upset she is one. I'm not saying it would help if she weren't one.

Pat: Why couldn't she tell me this?

Cc: She's an extremely shy girl, Pat, shy, sensitive, intelligent and intuitive.

Ed: So why can't she find a boyfriend?

Cc: She says the ones in her class are all too immature.

Ed: Immature? What does she think she is?

Pat: Ed, try to listen more and talk less.

Ed: Oh shut up. What about that guy who used to hang around the house all day, what's his name, Jonathan?

Pat: Jonathan has a boyfriend.

Ed: What?

Cc: She thinks she's the only one that doesn't have one.

Pat: So, we'll find her a boyfriend. I had no trouble finding them.

Cc: First I think she has to check into a detoxification center to take care of the drug problem. I know of one located very near here in an ashram. Now don't jump to conclusions about what an ashram is, it can be a real place for healing and for Zivia, a place to straighten herself out. I went there when I was having some problems a year ago. I was on the verge of a nervous breakdown and I was drinking too much.

Pat: You, Cc?

Ed: I told you that.

Pat: Ed's getting on my nerves today.

Cc: I've gotten Zivia to agree to talk to this man I know who works there. All I have to do is call him. I told Zivia it's just a place where people go to meditate and think things over.

Ed: I don't know if I go for this idea, an ashram. What's this guy like? How long would she be away for?

Cc: He's utterly harmless and the program can be as short as a

week depending on the concentration. Everything is done with
meditation. Now, Zivia's in there popping popcorn. All I have
to do is call the man from the ashram. Why are all the lights
and shades shut?

Pat: Ian did it. He says he's a vampire and that he did bite you
and liked it and wants a bag of blood from the butcher.

Cc: A vampire? Do you think I should call a psychiatrist?

Pat: A psychiatrist!—what for? He's agreed to work on Ed's play
and we're all going to be in it and have a backer's audition
right here in the living room.

Cc: Here?

Ed: Sure, we're going to pitch our tent outside until the show's
ready.

Cc: Ian really agreed to work on the play?

Ed: He's just going to polish it up a bit. He's going to be in it too,
the biggest part. We're all going to be in it, with VIPs
watching.

Cc: I can't really act, Ed.

Pat: I'm in it and I'm going to act. If I can act anyone can act.

Cc: What I really want to do is design. I designed this dress I'm
wearing. It's Dior-inspired, the New Look. *(Realizing she's
without the skirt section of the dress)* Where'd the rest of my
dress go?

Pat: Ian took it downstairs.

Cc: Downstairs? Anyway, I bet you're pretty surprised by what I'm
saying. I've never shown you anything but I've been sketching
fashions for years and then of course you know I've been
working the past year for that designer fellow, sewing and
helping out with odds and ends. Well, just from seeing his
work up close I've gotten so much more self-confident! I'm
really good, I'm better than he is—way better! Given a chance
I could make a name for myself. Let me do the costumes for
your show, Ed—I'll work day and night to get them done on
time—they'll be interesting and imaginative and respect your
text—costumes can make a show work on a whole different
level, Ed.

Ed: Sure, good idea.

Cc: Really?!

Ed: It's a great idea!

Cc: Pat, what do you think?

Pat: Yes, it's a good idea. I'd offer to help but I don't sew.

Cc: You know, Pat, I just thought of it in the kitchen, you should wear your hair in a chignon. Have you ever thought of it? It would look fantastic. I mean when it gets longer.

Pat: I'm going in the kitchen to talk to Zivia. *(She exits)*

Cc: I'm so happy. This could be just the break I need.

Ed grabs Cc and kisses her, rubbing his hands and body against her. She fights him away, thinking perhaps he's going to bite her too. She breaks away from him.

What's wrong with you! Are you crazy?! You must be crazy to grab me like that!

Ed: Oh don't pretend we've never held each other or kissed or did other things.

Cc: Are you talking about things that happened fifteen years ago because I think you are. Just because I'm enthusiastic about the chance to design costumes for your show doesn't mean the hands of the clock have fallen off.

Ed: We were together.

Cc: Don't turn it in your mind into some interesting illicit thing because it wasn't. It was before either of us were married, before I even considered marrying your brother or you met Pat.

Ed: You wanted me.

Cc: So what. Don't be such a cornball, Ed. Go pitch your tent, go on.

Ed: You better be careful, the Lash brothers are animals.

Ed makes, for fun, a wolflike face and growl and exits. Cc picks up the telephone and dials.

Cc: Hello, this is Cc Lash. That's right. Is Porter there? Could
you? Thanks.

*Cc opens the curtains and shade, filling the room again with
sunlight. From the window we can see Ed outside pitching his
tent. Cc takes out a first-aid kit and, with a gauze pad and
adhesive tape, bandages her neck where she has been bit.
This activity continues into her telephone conversation.*

Porter? Hi, it's Cc, how are you? I'm okay. I'm designing
costumes for a new show and I'm very excited about it.
Actually, Porter, I'm not calling about myself at all really. It's
about my niece, a striking girl. You'll be very impressed with
her. She's having some kind of drug problem and I thought
you could—no, I can't just send her over, you've got to come
here first, today. She's very shy and suspicious. I think you
owe me this much, Porter. It's a short drive, borrow a car. The
address is on the Rolodex.

*Enter Pat and Zivia with a long-handled popcorn popper
filled with popcorn.*

Well, Porter, see you very soon, good, bye. *(She hangs up)*
That was Porter.
Pat: Wasn't it a little early to call?
Cc: Oh they wake up and go to sleep very early there. Porter is
very clever and industrious. He's a very interesting young
man. I think you'll enjoy meeting him, Zivia. Maybe you'll
even decide you'd like to visit the place he works at after all.
How about if I make it Zivia Day ad hoc and you can have
anything you want for lunch, Zivia? What would you like, you
name it.
Zivia *(Eating popcorn)*: I'm not hungry.
Pat: Hamburger is Zivia's favorite.
Zivia: I'm not hungry.
Cc: Okay, you think about it while I go upstairs to change.

Zivia: Don't you want to hear the song I told you about?

Cc: When I come downstairs you'll play it for me, okay? *(She exits)*

Pat *(Cautious, maternal)*: What's the song you want to play, Ziv? I'd like to hear it, if you'd like to play it for me. Is it a song we can dance to? Do you remember you and I used to dance together, Zivia, when you were little? I liked that so much. Up to recently, Zivia, we've always been close. Why do you think we're not as close as we used to be, Zivia? Aunt C says you want a boyfriend.

Zivia: I don't want a boyfriend.

Pat: There's nothing wrong with wanting a boyfriend, Zivia. Having a boyfriend can be fun. And if you had one your father and I wouldn't be so worried about you taking drugs because you wouldn't—

Zivia: Stop saying I take drugs when I don't take them or I will just for spite!

Pat: All right, all right, these are just Michelle's, I believe you. But I'm going to have to talk to Michelle's father and tell him Michelle's using these harmful things.

Zivia: They're not Michelle's either. She's just keeping them for a friend too.

Pat: Okay, Zivia, we won't talk about it. Let me just take this stuff and flush it down the toilet.

Zivia: No, it's not mine. I have to give it back.

Pat: Zivia, possession of this stuff is completely illegal. You'll be doing your friend or Michelle's friend or whoever it is a big favor.

Zivia: Leave it. I'll throw it away myself. I dreamt about Axel before in the kitchen standing up awake. He was calling to me.

Pat: Please, Zivia, when you mention Axel to Mom you get me very, very upset.

Zivia: You said I could call you Pat instead of Mom.

Pat: If you want to you can, Zivia. I'd prefer you to call me Mom because that's a name we can have just between the two of us but if you want to call me Pat that's okay too.

Without warning, Zivia turns on the tape of Screamin' Jay Hawkins singing "I Put a Spell on You" at medium-loud volume. The tape begins immediately on the first line of the song. Pat listens. Zivia moves oddly to the music as she did previously. Screamin' Jay Hawkins sings: "I put a spell on you/ Because you're mine."

Zivia, lower it, your uncle's sleeping. *(Since Zivia doesn't move, she lowers the volume herself)* This is an old song. Where did you get this? I barely remember it. Sounds like a madman. In a good way. It's a love song.

Zivia: No.

Pat shuts off the stereo system. Zivia, not singing, continues to move to the now absent music.

Pat: I feel you're trying to tell me something, Zivia, am I right? Something in code? Something this song means to you.

Zivia: No.

Pat: Well then why did you just play that for me?

Zivia: I want to sing like him.

Pat: You know I love you very much, Zivia, more than anyone in the whole world and I'd do anything to make you happy. Tell me what would make you happy and go back to the way you used to be.

Zivia: I want to sing like Screamin' Jay Hawkins.

Pat: Well, that shouldn't be too difficult. How about it if I can convince Daddy to write into his play a place where you could sing a song?

Zivia: *This* song.

Pat: Yes, how would that be?

Zivia: It would have to be this one.

Pat: Okay, and then you'd be happy and you wouldn't take anything harmful to yourself or—

Zivia: I already said I don't.

Pat: Okay, I trust you and believe you and I'm going out to speak

to Daddy right now, okay? What are you going to do, listen to
music?

*Zivia makes an affirmative sound and turns on the tape
which plays again "I Put a Spell on You." Pat exits. Zivia
shuts the shade and curtains. Zivia, not at all desperately but
rather efficiently, tightens a cord around her arm and gives
herself an injection. When she is almost through, Ian calls
from the cellar.*

Ian *(Offstage)*: Where's my drink! I'm thirsty. Did somebody go to
the butcher? If somebody doesn't get me blood from the
butcher I'm going to start biting everyone. *(He enters, he is in
ordinary, striped pajamas as well as his improvised cape)* My
my my what have we here. So, you're a little drug addict,
Zivia; that's interesting.

Zivia: What?

Ian turns off the music.

Ian: Do you have a hit for me?

Zivia: I'm not doing anything.

Ian: I didn't say you were doing anything. I'm not doing anything
either except maybe looking for an early grave. I think maybe
you're looking for one too.

Zivia: Michelle's father is going to make a remake and he's going to
put Michelle and me in it.

Ian: How nice for you and your little friend. How old are you now,
Ziv, eight? nine? ten?

Zivia: Forty.

Ian: Oh, right, forty, that's a difficult transition year, forty. No
wonder you're at nerve's end.

Zivia: Did you know Jesus, Joseph and Mary are the same person?

Ian: No, I can't say I did. It's an original idea certainly, very
compact. Is it your own or something you picked up in Sunday
School?

Zivia: I don't go to Sunday School anymore. I teach it.

Ian: You teach Sunday School? Rich.

Zivia: I'm an assistant.

Ian: Only an assistant? Now, I would have thought you were a consultant of the high bishops or something like that. Takes time. Come to think of it, Zivia, you might be just the girl I'm looking for to debate good and evil. Because that's what I'm preoccupied with of late but my big problem is I can't find an intelligent soul to wrestle with. Won't you be my angel's advocate, Zivia, you being a Sunday School assistant and all?

Zivia *(Murkily)*: Where's the rewind? Is this the rewind?

Ian: Leave that for a while, Zivia, and sit down and have a debate with me. I think it would be great fun. Now, bear with me, I'm making this up as I go along. Don't nod out, Zivia, I need your participation! Now, it's my point of view that everyone on earth is after the transcendent state of being. In other words, everyone's trying to leave earth! I don't mean just astronauts, I mean everybody! This impulse to "transcend" comes from hating life. Are you with me? I'm sure I'm right. Now, in what ways do people try to transcend? Well, the first things that come to mind are alcohol, drugs—now there's something maybe you could help with, Ziv, you being a dabbler in mood-changing needlepoint and by way of that a knocker on the door of Doctor Death, in this case your pediatrician. Any comment, Ziv? What is this stuff anyway, heroin? Okay, you want to keep all your energy for your serve; I'll go along with that. Where was I? Alcohol, drugs, what else? War, war's a good one, war, general insurrection, criminal acts, definitely criminal acts and then of course art, sex and madness. Now, what I'd like to put forward to you, Zivia, maverick theocrat and celebrated Sunday School assistant that you are, is that evil—and I mean evil in the most antediluvian sense—that evil is the premier transcendent state of being. Now, you're sitting there so still and quiet because you're wondering what evil things did Uncle Ian do? Well, I provoked a bad actor to suicide but that, somehow I fear, was more a civic duty than an act of wickedness. Let's see, oh, then of course I called your dad's little marionette show a pea-brain's peephole into politics. But there again I was just serving truth. What else? I bit my wife. I considered biting your mother and I'll probably before you leave the room bite you. Now, I'm going to shut up and you argue an opposing point of view like goodness is all or drugs are king or I'm full of shit—it's your move, Zivia: speak.

Zivia: Michelle Frank's father has an Advent screen and showed us four episodes of "The Donna Reed Show" and he's going to combine and remake them and Michelle and I are going to have parts.

Ian: Stick to the material, Zivia.

Zivia: In one, Donna's son Jeff Stone saves a little girl from rolling off a bridge and the little girl's mother gives Jeff a sports car and Jeff gives it back so he won't get spoiled.

Ian: Oh, you're too clever for me, Ziv, these are parables, aren't they! Simple yet cryptic tales from which I must extract the nut of enlightenment, right?

Zivia: In the second one Donna's daughter Mary Stone is taken to college where she sings "Johnny Angel" and Donna realizes Mary's not a little girl anymore.

Ian: College in this case is meant to mean purgatory, right? And what Mary Stone realizes is indeed she's not a little girl anymore, she's a corpse! Even the name is perfect: Mary, Queen of Heaven, and Stone, lifeless object of the temporal world, and the superego, the actress, caught, if you will, like a reed between the two!

Zivia: Donna's husband, Doctor Stone, accuses Donna of being cheap because she keeps balls of tinfoil in her drawer so she dyes a dress for a big ball and tells him it's a new one.

Ian: The balls of tinfoil are lost souls, the dyed dress is redemption, the big ball: heaven, and Donna's fib, metaphysic-insemination!

Zivia: Donna joins a book club and is forced to read *War and Peace* by Leo Tolstoy even when she's vacuuming but in the

end she can't finish it and has to stand up and say so which
makes her husband proud and—

Ian: Enough, Zivia! Give me the answers to my questions!

Zivia: Michelle's father says all characters are interchangeable and
Donna could just as well be Diver Dan and he showed us a
tape to prove it and in it a fish named Baron Barracuda comes
to visit Diver Dan who—

Ian: The time, Zivia, for non sequiturs has come and gone. Give
me my answers! Answer anything but make it an answer
because, Zivia, I am desperate! I do not understand anything
anymore—I've got that old-fashioned bug: nausea—do you
know what that is, Zivia—I think maybe you do, so tell me
what is what, Zivia! I'll dance to your beat but be sure you
speak to me in clean clear directions! Tell me Satan will
appear with a giant shrimp fork and take me down into his
fiery spit or God and angels will have me whole with no sin or
bone left over! Put down your popcorn and listen to me or
goddamn you and everything I will sink my teeth into your
neck and suck out the answer!

Zivia (*Offhand*): My mother said you're a vampire.

Ian (*Hands up, practically shrieking*): I AM!

*Zivia bops Ian over the head with the iron popcorn skillet.
The popcorn springs up in the air and showers down. Ian
falls unconscious to the floor. Zivia, unmoved, turns on her
tape. Screamin' Jay Hawkins sings. Porter enters without
knocking. He is tall, thin, wears a dark, ill-fitting suit, white
wrinkled shirt and dark tie; this is his uniform. He is
ordinary.*

Porter: In high school, in college, in everyday life, people said,
Porter, drink this, I said okay, they said, smoke this, I said,
okay, they said, swallow this, I said okay, okay, okay. Then
was I in Mexico, was I in Tangiers, where was I? I was lost. I
was lost and my soul, for I had one yet, cried out okay. I
heard it quite distinctly for it was my evening of total

transfiguration and I said okay, I am lost, okay I am lost,
okay which is the way, okay I will pray, okay let prayer come,
okay. I threw down my needle for I was a substance abuser
and I threw down my bottle for I was a substance abuser and
I threw down my tired lonely lying face for I was a substance
abuser—

Zivia *(She turns off the music abruptly)*: In the kitchen behind the
door standing up awake I dreamt of my brother Axel calling to
me. My mother and my father say not to mention Axel because
he's lost.

Porter: Who can say he or she is not lost? Alone and afraid is lost.
Alone and afraid is lost. My voice is like a secret voice talking
out of your bones and it says oh I am tired oh I am worn out.
The morning, the night, I fall down to bed and what is the
answer, what is the question, God who is Vishnu. What is the
answer. God who is Vishnu. Okay. God. Okay. Vishnu. Okay.
Vishnu.

Zivia: My uncle's a vampire. He tried to bite me.

Porter: Okay. What cannot be subdued by the power of Vishnu?

Zivia: I just hit him over the head with the popcorn maker. Do you
know Jesus, Joseph and Mary are the same person?

Porter: Do you know Brahma, Vishnu and Shiva are the same
person?

Zivia: Do you know Diver Dan and Donna Stone are
interchangeable?

Porter: Do you know Krishna and Rama are interchangeable?

Zivia: Do you know where I can find my brother Axel?

Porter: Axel.

Zivia: My uncle named him.

Porter: You have the same last name as your aunt? That's the little
boy who disappeared at the beach about four years ago.

Zivia: Do you have him?

Porter: Whose house is this?

Zivia: My father says it's mine.

Porter: Come away with me to the ashram.

Zivia: I'm supposed to go to cross country where baby Jesus walks on hot stones in the desert while Mary holds a flashlight. I'm going to ask them to find me Axel and then we're going to live together in a house.

Porter: Wouldn't you rather come with me? I can help you find him.

Zivia: Do you know "I Put a Spell on You"?

Porter: Yes.

Zivia: By Screamin' Jay Hawkins?

Porter: Yes.

Zivia: By heart, inside out?

Porter: Yes.

Zivia: Do you want to hold my hand?

Porter: Yes.

Zivia: Say then you've been waiting for me all your life, prayed for me, me and not the others, me and me and me alone.

Porter (*On one knee*): Yes, of course.

They kiss.

END OF ACT ONE

*A week later. Afternoon. Ed and Pat are wearing costumes Cc
has designed for Ed's show. They are broadly patriotic,
theatrical costumes in red, white and blue stars and stripes.
The silhouette is Betsy Ross. The fabric is matte cotton, not
spangled or glittery. Pat has a large, hooped, red-and-white
striped skirt with a blue-and-white starred blouse. Ed is still
waiting for Cc to finish the combination shirt and waistcoat of
his costume. He is hammering, sawing and otherwise
finishing-up building a coffin shaped in the old-fashioned
wide-at-the-middle style but in many ways resembling a
kitchen cabinet.*

Pat: Tell me how old I am, Ed. Tell me. I'm thirty-three. Thirty-
three years old. That's two full years younger than she is and
she has the nerve—the temerity—to strike up a conversation
with me about eyelifts. As if I would ever need one for ten or
fifteen years! Who is she kidding, projecting her own aging
fears on me? When Zivia and I go out shopping together—you
don't know because you never take us—when we go out
shopping together the clerks always say, "Maybe your sister
wants to try one on too,"—your sister—meaning *me*.
They think we're sisters. I'm not talking about once; this
happens constantly. I look *that* young. Eyelifts! Then the one
about the conditioner. You were in the room, Ed. You were
there when she brought up the conditioner. Stop banging! I

don't need a conditioner and I don't need anyone to tell me I
do when I don't even if I did!

Ed: When somebody offers you advice, Pat, take it in the spirit it's
offered in. Don't go in search of imagined insults.

Pat: Oh, is that so?! Imagined insults? Like when she told you to
stop eating with your hands and tracking dirt through the
house with your shoes? That was all imaginary I suppose.

Ed: I can rise above that sort of thing. I'm not petty, Pat.

Pat: And I am? Because that's what you're saying. You know
something, Mister Lash, I'm getting a little bit fed up with
you, your brother and your brother's wife. I've been very
patient. I've sat and I've waited but I've seen no script. Today
is the day the VIPs or whatever-they-are are supposedly
supposed to come and—

Ed: What do you mean "supposedly"—they're coming.

Pat: Oh I've been told they've been invited but no RSVPs from a
big bunch of people?—that's very strange. We've had no
rehearsal. You haven't seen it at all. We're supposed to just
leap up and do it impromptu?

Ed: He's giving it to me today, any minute. We don't need to
rehearse. The spontaneity will keep it fresh.

Pat: Yeah? And why aren't you working on it together? Why hasn't
he even asked you for the time of day?

Ed: That's just the way Ian works.

Pat: You're a very trusting soul, Ed, that's all I've got to say, to
trust so absolutely a man who called your play, and I quote,
"babyish." I'll tell you, I've kept my tongue curbed. I've told
myself, wait, don't judge too quickly but now I feel I can keep
my silence no longer. I am compelled to tell you exactly what I
think about these costumes: they are absurd! They are
ridiculous, Ed! They will make your play into a big fat joke!

Ed: The costumes are fine, they're imaginative.

Pat: Ed, they're ridiculous. Do you know what that word means,
Ed? People will laugh at them!

Ed: They're a little outlandish but that's part of her concept. It
puts the play on a whole different level.

Pat: That it does!

Ed: I'm not going to let you spoil the good feeling I have. I'm just going to tell myself you're cranky, Pat, and let it go at that.

Pat: Maybe I wouldn't be so cranky if I hadn't slept all week on a leaky air mattress in a drafty tent!

Ed: Well, after today we go home.

Pat: Hallelujah!

Ed: Try and understand what all this means to me, Pat. It's a dream come true. I've sunk all my ideas into this play. It's everything I believe in. I have faith in it—I believe it can reach out and speak to other people.

Pat: Ed, I've heard all this. Tell me exactly what your highest hopes are with this thing?

Ed: I want my parents to see it.

Pat: *What?!* Those two *creeps!*

Ed: Look, Pat, you and my folks have nothing in common so there's no point in deriding them. They mean a lot to me. I love them. They're my parents. All their lives they've put a lot of emphasis on intellectual achievement and their gods have always been artists. My mother said there's no greater gift to man a man can make than a sonnet or a concerto.

Pat *(Disbelief)***:** *Her?*

Ed: And my father agrees totally.

Pat: So why didn't you have them come to the reading?

Ed: I knew it wasn't ready. I wanted it to be just right, to combine the humanitarian impulse with aesthetic achievement which is the secret of greatness. Ian knows this, he does. He's known it since he was little so my parents have always favored him—understandably—and nurtured the possibility that he would turn out to be an artist and make a contribution to society.

Pat: Ed.

Ed: So things haven't worked out that way and I'm picking up the task. But do you know something? I'm better than Ian could ever be and do you know why? Because the whole time Ian was in the house with his nose stuck in books I was outside

mixing with people. I know people! Ian says my business is
wood; it's not, it's people.

Pat: Ed.

Ed: So no one can accuse me of not standing behind my brother —
I have. I thought to myself, Ian's carrying the burden, it's my
job to help him out and if that means dipping into my pocket:
okay.

Pat: What?

Ed: I paid for this house.

Pat: *Are you trying to blow my mind?!*

*Enter Cc with Ed's combination shirt-waistcoat. It is similarly
of the stars-and-stripes motif. Cc wears her play costume:
Dior influenced perhaps, reinterpreted in red, white and blue.
She has a small pointed matching hat for Pat.*

Cc: I have your waistcoat, Ed, but you're going to have to wait a
few minutes for the belt and hat. I'm doing all those last but I
have yours, Pat.

Pat: Thanks.

Cc: The costumes are coming out amazing, aren't they?

Pat: They definitely are.

Cc *(To Ed)*: How does it fit? Tight or loose?

Ed: It's just right.

Cc: Try on your hat, Pat.

Pat: Couldn't I wait until later?

Cc: But if it fits funny I can make adjustments now.

Pat: Haven't you done enough?

Cc: What's that, Ed? What are you building?

Ed: It's a coffin for the show. Ian said it was the one necessary
prop.

Cc: You spoke to him? Did he say anything about his costume, that
he liked it?

Ed: No, just build a coffin.

Cc: Well, be sure you sand it well so none of the costumes catch on
it and rip. I better get back in the kitchen and finish. The

sewing machine's on its last leg but somehow after today I feel I'm not going to need this old machine anymore. *(She exits)*

Pat: Her dress is even worse than mine. It wouldn't seem possible.

Ed: Maybe I should tell her to make them a little more subtle. She could dye them. Dyeing's cheap, isn't it?

Pat: Do you mean to tell me point blank this house is ours and we've been sleeping in a tent in the driveway?

Ed: Legally the house will go eventually to Zivia. I don't want to discuss it. It's something between brothers you can't understand.

Pat: I have a brother.

Ed: Between *men*, Pat. You're not a man, are you?

Pat *(Making a short sound by pursing her lips and blowing out air)***:** Men! Brothers! All that means is more competitive, more jealous, more rivalry.

Ed: Subject closed.

Pat: It's your subject.

Ed *(Hammering each syllable)***:** I don't want to discuss it.

Pat: What besides your play have you wanted to discuss, Ed? Not Zivia. Have you counted how many times this week you've wondered how she's doing?

Ed: It wasn't my idea to send her there and if anything goes further wrong with her I'm holding you responsible.

Pat: You want a divorce, Ed? I'll give you one.

Enter Ian considerably improved, happier and better groomed. He is similarly attired à la Fourth of July. As a result of Zivia's assault his head is bandaged in white gauze; even this happily conjures the American Revolution.

Ian: Ed, Pat, I have a glorious announcement and some apologies. The first apology is to you, Ed. Your play I completely misjudged and I love it now. I love it top to bottom. It's brilliant. It's superb. I adore it.

Ed: You really like it?

Ian: I do, Ed, I do. I underestimated you and I'm sorry. I sat in

the basement all week and I read your play over and over and
over again and do you know what happened?

Pat: What?

Ian: I discovered its core!

Ed: You did? Where is it?

Ian: What?

Ed: The script.

Ian: Oh, here. *(He hands Ed the radically thinned text)*

Pat: That looks like just the core.

Ed: What's happened to it?

Ian: It's essentialized now.

Ed: Well, I guess I have to read it. I better go to the tent so I can
concentrate.

Ian: Okay, Ed, see you later.

Ed exits reading quizzically.

Pat: Ian, I think about Axel, more now than when he first
disappeared. I feel anxious and guilty all the time even though
I didn't do anything wrong. I need to talk about it and Ed
won't.

Ian: Guilt is an abstraction, Pat. If you don't let it exist it won't.
Look at me. Don't I seem happier and better adjusted than
last week? People were trying to make me feel guilty because of
that actor's suicide. What no one knows is that he had written
to me several times asking for my advice about coming out of
semiretirement to play that role. I said, sure, why not? So,
after I gave him the review he deserved, he wrote me this long
frantic letter about how he was finished blah-blah-blah and
was going to take his own life. Now, Pat, was it my place to
step in and try to prevent him from doing what he had set his
mind on doing? I don't think so.

Pat: You really think Ed's play is good, that it'll make money?

Ian: Oh, it won't make any money. It's not that kind of thing.

Pat: Oh. Ian, sit and talk with me a few minutes. I'm worried about Zivia. Let me rest my head for a second on your shoulder.

Ian: I have to tell Cc I'm better and that I'm sorry I bit her.

Pat: Couldn't we just exchange tendernesses for a moment, nothing sexual, just tenderness. I'm very nervous.

Ian: She's upstairs, isn't she? I'll go check and I'll come back.

Ian exits upstairs swiftly. Pat cries for a moment, catches herself at it and stops: it's not in her character and makes her uncomfortable. She draws the shades and curtains. The room is considerably darkened. Enter Cc with a hat.

Cc: I have Ed's hat. It's so dark in here. Pat?

Pat: I'm over here. Don't open the curtains, my eyes hurt.

Cc: What's wrong?

Pat: Nothing's wrong. Ian came up from the basement with the play and Ed took it into his tent to read.

Cc: Was Ian wearing his costume?

Pat: Yes. He said he's sorry he bit you.

Cc: He is? He said that?

Pat: Yes.

Cc: Then everything's going well.

Pat: What do you really think of Ed's script?

Cc: Think of it? I don't think anything of it. It's good.

Pat: I've always found it rather stupid and couldn't figure out Ed's obsession with it. He makes so much money at his own job, why this interest in another profession? If anyone I've always thought Ian would eventually become a writer, he's been everything else it seems and he has so many opinions on how things should be. Ed's job is so lucrative, you see.

Cc: Why are you stressing money so much? People have to do what will make them happy in the end.

Pat: Nothing, just that I'm tired of sleeping outside in a tent when actually in reality this house is ours!

Cc: What are you saying, Pat?

Pat doesn't answer.

I know Ian has gotten some loans from his brother during rough times but that's between them. I don't even know how much—

Pat: We paid for this house.

Cc: No.

Pat: Yes. It's a fact.

Cc: But Ed can't make that much money. Maybe he helped a little bit but—

Pat: Ed is a cabinetmaker. Do you know how much it costs to put cabinets in if you don't have any or change the cabinets you have if you want new ones? *A lot.*

Cc: Ian made some extra money he said writing some longer articles.

Pat: Don't make me laugh! Ian is a pauper.

Cc: Then this isn't even our home.

Pat: You got it. That's what's so annoying—all your airs about art, furniture, clothing and hair and all when it's our money.

Cc: Pat, I paid for many of these things with my own money. I work.

Pat: Work? Sewing roses on dresses with the stereo on is not work, my dear, it's a hobby, a pastime—*I work!*

Cc: You're a cashier.

Pat *(Shaking with rage)*: How dare you call me a cashier! *How dare you?!*

Cc *(Defensive, frightened)*: Isn't that what you are? Well, what are you?

Pat: I'm an accountant!

Cc: Okay, so you're an accountant there too but you do work the cash register. I didn't know you did the books too.

Pat *(Out of breath)*: My only objective in coming here was that the two brothers be reconciled but—and I would've kept my tongue but you've pressed me—your husband has made some unignorable passes at me.

Cc: Ian's been in the basement!

Pat: He came up from the basement and made very clear sexual passes at me. Why are you so disbelieving—you don't think I'm good-looking enough? I most certainly am! I know you think you have such good taste but you don't have such good taste. My friends would laugh at what you consider good taste. And you think your figure's so good? Let me tell you, it's not as good as you think it is. You think you're such an interesting person but you're not so interesting.

Cc: Are you quite through?

Pat: No—are you?—of dropping all your backbiting, little helpful hints? Diet? Dye job? Moisturizers? Which is it? Tell me all at once and get it over with, you're such an expert! That's the trouble with us, Cc, you're a know-it-all and I'm a know-it-all and neither of us wants to know what the other one knows so that's why we can't become friends. And I don't need a conditioner—you do! You lighten it and you lighten it and it has no luster—get me?!

Cc: Pat—

Pat: Don't think I don't know where all this animosity comes from because I do—you loving Ed. I know that you've always been in love with him—you thought I didn't know that! But what *you* don't know is that your marriage was arranged—arranged by Ed and Ian's parents. You were given to Ian because they felt the older son should be married first and they worried about Ian anyway—he wasn't dating anyone, he was cynical about everything and to top it all off they found him effeminate! So you got him!

Cc: This can't be true.

Pat: Oh no? What can be more true?! Ed—good little son that he is—went along with his parents and broke off the engagement with you. So, girlie, next time you bring up eyelifts look to your own eyes because there's nothing wrong with mine!

Pat exits to the kitchen. Porter enters from the front door. He looks the same as he did in Act One.

Porter: World existence tugs at us and tugs at us until we feel surely we will be taken down and crushed under the mighty weight of its steamroller. See the fog it casts? Sit perfectly still and chant: Om namo deva devesha paraatpara jagadguro.

Cc: I don't want to chant, Porter. Where's my niece?

Porter: She's in the car. You've stopped chanting, why?

Cc: Because I stopped understanding why I was doing it or even what it was so it all started to sound like mumbo jumbo to me. Is Zivia better?

Porter: What it is is a sword to hack through the real mumbo jumbo of worldliness which of course is the hypnotic hiss of the dragon forever guarding the door so we may not escape to illumination, grace and purification. We pass through the door by the exalting rigor of devotion. Only there, salvation. Zivia and I want to start our own ashram. We thought perhaps this house.

Cc: This house? An ashram?

Porter: Zivia and I are in love.

Cc: Are you crazy?

Porter: Poor Cc. I know you still love me. Love is the petrification of a hunger.

Cc: No, it's not, Porter, and I'm not in love with you and never have been. I came to you when I was in a very vulnerable position. I was having a nervous breakdown. You were of no help whatsoever but at the time I believed you sincerely wanted to help. I paid you back by lending you I don't know how much money, none of which you've returned. Now, if there's some way you can help my niece, great, I'll forget your debt but don't come panhandling around my life a second time. Please have that much shame and human decency.

Porter: It's you now who aren't listening. Listen instead to a story of horror. You ask me where is Zivia. Ask instead where is her brother Axel. He is at the beach but he is not swimming. He is under the sand. Where did I hear this story? From a priest who had to suffer its details during a confession. From what mouth sprang this tale? None other than the child's own mother. Yes! The mother and the father sat on the off-season beach reading magazines. The child, unnoticed, strolled down to the water's edge, drowned there, was discovered by the parents who screamed, cried, hit each other and eventually stuck the small body in a hole they dug with their fingers in the sand. Why, because they were afraid people would say they killed their own child or would believe as much and call it negligence. Hence the make-believe disappearance of baby Axel.

Cc: That's not true—that's made up.

Porter: Every word of it is true. I married Zivia. We're married.

Cc: She's under age. She's a child. You can't marry her. It's illegal.

Porter: Zivia holds the title of this house in trust. As her husband and guardian the house is now mine. It will be turned into an ashram. What you don't know, C, is that Zivia has become a mystic. She is at one with the power of God. The people at the ashram recognized her immediately as a Madonna figure and soon, stunned by her powers, they fell to their knees in supplication. The number of her devotees doubles as we stand here now.

Cc: What powers?

At the front door there is a knocking so loud it rattles the house. The door, slowly and with a creak, opens. It is Zivia. She enters. She is in a state of otherness but not particularly different from before. Her hair is cut shorter. Pat, having heard the knocks, enters.

Pat: Zivia, you're back. I missed you so much. Can I give you a kiss and a hug? How are you feeling, honey, better? You've cut your hair. It's very nice. Did you get thinner? You can't afford to get thinner, Ziv. Didn't they feed you over there? What's wrong, baby?

Cc: Zivia, how are you? Wait until you see the costume I made for you. I think you're going to love it. It's an Indian costume.

Zivia: A sari?

Cc: No, an American Indian.

Zivia *(Meaninglessly)***:** Oh.

Pat: That's fun, Zivia, isn't it? Look at my costume. Isn't it funny? Zivia, talk to me. Tell me what it was like, what did you do?

Zivia: The first morning I made a broom out of straw. Then I swept the floor. Then I scrubbed it.

Pat: Well, if that just doesn't beat everything! At home I can't even get you to wipe the counter. Zivia, you're a riot! What did you have for breakfast?

Zivia: Rice. Then I rang the bell.

Pat: Rice? You don't like rice. Rice with what?

Zivia: Rice alone.

Porter: Go upstairs and rest for a short while, we have a lot of work to do.

Cc: I left the costume on my bed, Ziv. You can go and try it on, see if it fits.

Zivia exits to upstairs.

Pat: She looks like hell. What did you do to her over there? And what do you mean telling her "we've got a lot of work to do"? What work? My daughter doesn't scrub floors. I don't trust you. What's your name again?

Porter: I'm your daughter's husband.

Pat: Her husband? Husband. Is that slang for something? Have you fucked my daughter? I mean I don't even want to ask, Buster—I mean my husband will kill you and I don't mean that figuratively—I mean you'll be dead.

Porter: We're married.

Pat: Is this a joke, Cc? I've always wondered what you find funny; is this your joke? Married? Even for a joke, even just to say it—do you have any idea how old she is? Do you know what statutory rape is? Tell me, do you know, do you know what it is, statutory rape and how many years you'll be locked up— you'll be too old to focus before you see unstriped sunlight again!

Porter: Perhaps we'll share prison facilities.

Pat: What did you say to me? What did he say? Is he on drugs?

Cc: Leave it alone. Pat.

Pat: Listen, mister, you are playing with the wrong lady, hit the road!

Ed enters. His costume is ripped and dirtied. He holds a book.

Cc: Ed! What happened to your costume!

Ed: Nothing. I just read Ian's great secret rewrite and then caught him trying to escape down the trellis.

Cc: Oh, Ed!

Pat: You didn't kill him, did you? I told you not to trust him!

Ed: What are you saying, Pat? One can't just kill a vampire—they might have a comeback. You've got to use some foolproof technique. So, here, out of Ian's own trash can I've found the prescription for his problem. Look, the book opens right to the page!

Cc: Ed.

Ed: "The way to prepare a vampire is to chop off his head, stuff the mouth with garlic—

Pat: Sounds like a cookbook.

Ed: —and drive long nails through the skull."

Pat: Ed, get him to write the retraction like I told you.

Cc: Ed, we'll do the original text. Don't worry about it. Take off your costume so I can mend it.

Ed: We can't do the original one—thanks to Ian, it's already been laughed at!

Cc: The costumes will make it seem different.

Ed: The costumes have to be cut. I'm sorry, Cc, but they're just plain silly. Take them out into the light of day and I'm sure you'll agree.

Cc: Cut? Do you know how many hours I've put in these costumes, how much of myself? Everybody's restless, tired, overworked and nervous so we're jumping to unnecessary conclusions. I'm

going to bring out a nice big pot of tea and then we can all sit
down and talk over everything calmly. *(She exits to the
kitchen)*

Ed *(Gesturing to Porter)*: Who's this character?

Pat: This guy, Ed, is the guy from Cc's ashcan and—

Ed *(To Porter)*: Don't you talk? Don't you say hello?

Enter Ian, bloodied nose and lip, costume ripped.

Ian: Ed—don't hit me again! Can't we talk? Let's talk. I didn't
change it as a joke I swear to you I think it's better now. It is!

Ed: It's not mine!

Ian: It is, it's just cut and shortened a little bit.

Ed: If I thought it needed a barber I would've taken it to one.

Ian: Ed.

Ed: And these Halloween costumes—I'll bet you had something to
do with them, didn't you?

Ian: No, but they're not so terrible. They give it a nice German
Expressionist touch.

Ed: I don't want it to be German Expressionist—I want it to be
American! Naturalist!

Ian: Ed.

Ed: You must think I'm pretty stupid, Ian, don't you? "Dumb
Ed." Don't you think I know what you're trying to do? To take
credit away from me so Mommy and Daddy think you did it,
that it's your thing and not mine?

Ian: Oh, Ed!

Ed: *Oh Ed*—balls! How different is this from any time growing up
with you—with you in every instance working to make me look
bad, to make me look like the dumb one and—until I got
taller—the short one too! Daddy and I are the same height—
how come you're not? Because you've never wanted to grow
up—not literally or figuratively! And Mommy and Daddy out
of their innate goodness have kept their fingers crossed against
all odds that you would just one day cross that finishing line
without whining or crying or anyone else's push or crutch and

make them proud for one minute but you've done nothing but discourage, dishearten and disgust those two good souls!

Ian: Two good souls? There are certain things, Ed, I've kept from you—the four-year difference made a lot more difference when you were crib-bound—let's just leave it at that.

Ed: Leave what at that? You haven't said anything—you never do—only innuendo and slurs—this one no doubt about—

Ian: Ed, when you were a little thing wetting your bed, do you know what house chore was mine?

Ed: You can bet this will be a lie!

Ian: During the week, in the afternoons, I was put in the front room and told to cry out if anyone came in the house. Why? Oh, probably because Mr. Chin from across the street had just popped in and Mommy and he were playing rollover in the bedroom.

Ed: Liar! Bastard! Weakling!

Ian: And if that weren't enough—a mother setting up her five-year-old as a sentinel!—on the weekends, when it was Dad's turn to babysit and Mom was out shopping and lunching, Daddy would shuttle in Mrs. Young from around the block and once again I was positioned to play lookout and guard in the front room and commanded to cry out if anyone came home. When I listened I thought they were suffocating each other. I was terrified. You were asleep in your crib!

Ed: I'm going to stick you in this coffin so you can lie in your own shit for eternity!

Ian: I don't want to hurt you, Ed. I know how much they mean to you but look at them realistically, how they pitted us against each other—how were we ever to become friends?

Ed *(To Porter)*: What are you looking at?

Porter: You.

Ed: Is that so? Who the fuck are you?

Porter *(He is sitting placidly on the couch)*: My mother left my father and her sons to go to Hawaii. My father placed my brother and me in seminary school. My brother hung himself. I left the seminary and took hallucinogens. Hallucinogens led

Harry Kondoleon

me to my mother in Maui where she collapsed in an alcoholic stupor. There I experienced the first of many visitations. The visitations were difficult to interpret because I was so heavily cloaked in hate, hate with all my soul and being for everyone but especially people very much like yourselves. It was not unusual for me to look at someone and imagine them slowly burning as they struggled against the wires securing them to a dead tree or telephone pole. Somehow in the crackle of that fire a voice became more and more distinct, a voice that told me God's name over and over in all its manifestations. Of course then I knew my calling was to dedicate myself to God.

Ed: Is this guy for real?

Pat: You haven't heard the half of it.

Ian: Maybe the costumes confused me and threw me on the wrong track. Let's go back to the old way and I'll do it happily, Ed. All I want to do is help and for us not to fight, okay?

Ed: And you'll be in it in front of the VIPs?

Ian: What do they matter? What are they anyway but a pack of nobodies pretending to be somebodies.

Ed: They're somebodies to me and I want them here.

Ian: That's just an illusion.

Ed *(Equal stress on each word, slowly)*: Not to me.

Ian: The important thing, Ed, is to express yourself to the fullest as you've attempted to do—and succeeded! That's all the fulfillment we can expect in life—whether that be through your work or family or whatever! Shouldn't that be enough without expecting anyone to understand what brings each of us happiness?

Enter Cc with a silver tray with a silver tea service and china teacups and saucers.

Cc: Who wants cream and who wants lemon?

Ian: C, we all decided against the costumes. Nice try, but they're just a miss. Now, let's come up with a substitution. Street clothes? How about that, street clothes?

160

Cc *(Putting down the tea tray)*: The costumes are staying.

Ian: They don't work for what Ed wants, Cc. We have to think of him.

Cc: *The costumes stay.*

Ian: Cc, what we're trying to tell you is that they're not right. They're bad.

Pat *(Half under her breath)*: Yeah, they suck.

Cc: They're not bad, they're good. Extremely good. How do I know they're good? Because I know, *myself.* I'm no longer relying on yours or anyone else's opinion—you don't know what an emancipation that is!

Ian: Well, I'm glad for you.

Cc: No you're not. How could you be? You've never encouraged me in anything I've ever tried to do.

Ian: You never encouraged me in my painting.

Cc: Ever see Ian's oils, Pat? If you've never laughed out loud it would be your opportunity. And the one time I showed you my dress sketches you held them like dog turds. At least I'm trying to believe in what I do—what are you doing, Ian—I mean aside from bleeding me, what is your ambition?

Ed: She's mad because you said something about her costumes.

Cc: And teaching? Why couldn't you keep your teaching position at the college? The commitment was miniscule, small classes, short hours.

Ian: I hated my students.

Cc: Of course you did! You hate everyone!

Ian: Honestly now, Cc, how can you expect me to take these costumes seriously? They remind me of those greeting cards you used to design.

Cc: Odd you should mock that or any attempt I made to earn us some income when your job—when you had one!—was bringing in so little! And I wouldn't have minded any of the career switches—if that was your attitude about work—fine— but you specifically said you didn't want to have any children because you wanted to concentrate on your career. Which career? What career?! You made me lie to everyone that I couldn't have children—that I tried and couldn't! I can and I wanted them—I want them still!

Pat: Oh my.

Ian: Oh, the pity factor now.

Cc: What are you, Ian, anyway, but a little heap of useless opinions?

Ian: You mustn't hate me, Cc. It's not worth it.

Cc: Why shouldn't I hate you?! You bit me! No one has ever bit me! Not even a dog!

Pat: He's a vampire.

Ian: Maybe I'm not. Maybe I was only pretending to be one.

Cc: Pretending? If you bit someone and sucked their blood then you are one—there's nothing to pretend!

Ed: I don't know what you mean by street clothes. Except for the Indian I wanted them all in normal clothes.

Cc: My costumes are in! They stay in! They're the best thing in this show!

Ian: In, out, what difference does it make anyway. I didn't invite anyone. I threw all the invitations behind the boiler.

Ed: *You what?!*

Cc: You don't really think I trusted him, do you, Ed? I wrote each one a note demanding they come and I signed your name, Ian—not the first time I've done such a thing and several times if you recall at your request.

Ed: Good for you, Cc!

Cc *(To Ed)*: Get your filthy, lecherous hands away from me! Was there even one day this week you didn't appear at the kitchen door without that thing dangling out of your pants, begging, "Touch it—hold it—kiss it!"

Pat: *What am I hearing?!*

Ed: Sour grapes.

Cc: He probably thinks he owns me—he owns this house—I was a fool to ever think you could pay for it!

Ed *(To Pat)*: You told her that?!

Cc: You're going to hit her? Why not, it's your style. My husband

bites me, yours might as well hit you. I don't need a divorce—
I need a tetanus shot!

Ian: This is good, C. Don't you see, we can all live now without
illusions.

Cc: "Without illusions"—don't you think I've needed illusions to
live with you?!

Ian: The reason I didn't want children—aside from the fact they're
little noise boxes—is that I didn't want to solidify a
relationship when in the back of my mind I always vaguely
hoped a better one would come along and I would have that.

Cc: You've never loved me?

Ian: Oh, wouldn't it be nice to achieve whatever there is to achieve
in this life once and for all and get it over with so there would
be nothing left? Loved you? No, I didn't. There, I've said it.
Chew it over in your brain and digest it. I don't love you and I
never did: *fin*. My goodness!—most people would have gotten
the message by now!

*Cc, wolflike, growls, runs toward and leaps up at her
husband's throat. Ian tries to ward her off. If she falls she
springs to her feet to bite again. Ian screams. Pat and Ed
yank her off of him. There is blood on his neck and blood on
her mouth and chin.*

Pat: Oh God.

Ian: Bitch! Stupid bitch! She bit me!

Cc: When I was sixteen I went to a florist and bought one of every
flower with money I saved from my birthday and I burned
those flowers at an altar to love I constructed of loose bricks
behind the garage at midnight. I prayed that one day I would
be blessed with true love. I challenged the deities. I said deny
me good fortune, good health and random pleasures but grant
me a love so pure I could wake each morning in the state of
bliss and grace and fall down asleep at night wrapped in arms
that loved me! Look at me now. *(She rips off the bandage. Her*

neck is black and blue and yellow and red and looks infected.
Not pausing) Look at my neck!

Porter laughs a long laugh.

Porter: You crack me up, Cc. Walking backwards up the hill to
God! Oh it is so freeing to expect so little from the people you
meet! I used to be so deceived by people like you, by the fake
beats of your hearts! Now I know you are the small struggling
flies on the spoiling meat of this world. You flit upwards briefly
but return always to the steaming shit and you think you are
free! You came to the ashram. I said to myself this woman is
starving, she is ready to cut into God. But no, your pockets
were stuffed with chocolates to gorge yourself when the lights
went out. But I tell you it is in the dark God shows his terrible
face and we need both our hands to hold out, to hold out and
touch the sharp features! The blood on your hands, what is it
but your ticket! And what does the ticket say?—ABANDON
THIS WORLD.

Ed: I don't like this guy one iota.

Cc: I used to ask you who were we praying to—Vishnu? Buddha?
Jesus? Every day it got more and more vague. Was it even
God? And you'd say, well, not God, per se. What's an ashram
anyway but just another place to keep tidy?

Ed: I asked you before who you were and I want an answer.

Cc: He's a charlatan, a thief, an imposter, a seducer and a
puppeteer.

Porter: I'm your son-in-law.

Pat: I would say this is just about your last chance to run out that
door.

Porter: Mr. Lash, when your daughter came to us a
transformation occurred rendering her available to the unseen
world. She was recognized immediately by the people there as
a Madonna figure.

Ian: A McDonald's figure?

Cc: What he's trying to say, Ed, is because he borrowed money

from me but not enough and tried to seduce me but failed, he
has as an alternative seduced your daughter in the hope of
getting our home which you signed over to Zivia and turning it
into his own ashram which would be his own little house of
tidiness as if tidiness were spirituality or God something that
could be put on like a wrinkled business suit!

Ed: Are you trying to tell me he fucked my daughter?

Cc: That's right, Ed—get him!

Ed *(Grabbing Porter)*: All right, windbag, you've got two seconds
to pray.

Porter: Abandon this world or be doomed to return forever to it.

Pat: You'll be abandoning this world soon enough when my
husband punches you to death.

Porter: I don't suppose God, the police or the press know. Shall
we tell them, Ed? Pat?

Ed: What is he talking about?

Pat: He's talking about statutory rape. Punch him, Ed!

Porter: You despise me because I'm goodness—yes, goodness—
what else could I be?

Cc: He is so full of shit!

Porter: Aren't you thirsty, Cc? You used to drink quite a bit. Why
don't you have a drink?

Cc: Good idea! Why don't I?! *(She takes out a bottle and, tipping
it over vertically, drinks directly from it)* Punch him!

Ed: Give me that.

Ed takes a swallow of alcohol and passes the bottle to Pat.

Ian: Drinking alone? *(He grabs the bottle from Pat)* It's one of the
seven signs of alcoholism. *(He drinks)*

Porter: Look at yourselves! Find a mirror that will make your
reflection and look, you who have lost your souls—

Ian: Don't even complete your metaphor. Punch him, Ed.

*Ed punches Porter hard in the face. They all punch Porter
until he is unconscious.*

Stick him in the coffin.

Ed: Yeah, let him wake up in there. He'll think he died.

Pat: He deserves to. Then he'll know what it's like to be a real deadhead.

They stick Porter in the coffin.

Cc: Chanting and praying God God God and then you wake up in the night crazy with dissatisfaction and God laughs in your face—I know I have heard that laughing! *(She slams the lid shut)*

Ian: This is great, we've achieved solidarity by overthrowing a common enemy! It's silly for us to argue among ourselves—don't you see, we only have each other in the void.

Pat: What void?

Cc: Why not try to fill it, Ian, instead of just drawing attention to it?

Ian *(Sarcasm)*: Fill the void myself?

Ed: Yeah, get a job!

Pat: Where's the coffee? This is tea. I want coffee!

Cc: Coffee makes us nervous and agitated.

Pat: It doesn't make me nervous or agitated—I want my coffee!

Cc *(With moral weight)*: The tea is herbal.

Pat: You know, I never take any of your insults to heart, C, like when you sent us napkin rings as a wedding present.

Cc: They were sterling.

Pat: Or came to our house and only ate small portions.

Cc: You can't cook.

Pat: Or when I had my hair hennaed and Ed told me Ian told him you told Ian I looked like a jack-o'-lantern.

Cc: Ian said that!

Ian: Do you know what she made me do when we got married? Shave my shoulders! Said I looked like a werewolf!

Cc: You did; you still do.

Ian: Otherwise you wouldn't make love to me.

Cc: Make love to you? What does that mean?—give you blow jobs?—that's all you ever want to do anyway.

Pat: Ed too.

Ed: While we're on the subject, I'll tell you why you shortened my play, Ian—because my cock is longer than yours, that's why!

Ian: That's ridiculous.

Cc *(Pointedly)*: Is it?

Ed: What I'd like to know is where the hell is the TV in this room? I mean where is it hidden? I say there's something wrong with two people who have a TV and hide it!

Pat: *Why didn't you come to our wedding?!*

Ed: Logistically these are our—*my* things. If I want to break this, I can. And I do.

Ed puts his fist through a small painting of subway graffiti. Cc screams.

Pat: That affects her!—anything superficial! But when I asked her to help me pick out deck lamps for the pool—nothing!

Ed: What gets me is the way she's been looking down her nose all these years and then she comes out with these ridiculous costumes.

Cc: If they're so ridiculous don't wear them—take them off! *(She rips Ed's, Pat's and Ian's costumes)*

Ian: That's unnecessary, Cc.

Cc: Take them off—you're not fit for them—hypocrites and murderers! Oh don't look so shocked! And you, Ian, you think you're so shrewd that you always get to the bottom of things! Well, have you been to the bottom of the beach? You might find your godson there!

Pat *(She screams and begins hitting Ed wildly)*: You told her that! It's not true!

Cc: Not true? Completely true! *(On the word* him *she points at the closed coffin)* You told a priest and the priest told him and he told me!

Ed *(Hitting Pat)*: I told you not to go to confession!

Ian: They killed Axel?

Cc: They were reading magazines! Can you beat it!

Ian: And he drowned?

Cc: Bingo!

Ed: It was an accident—an accident can happen to anybody. Don't blow it up out of proportion.

Cc: And then they buried him!

Ian: And pretended he was lost!—it's a regular plot!

Pat: I went back. I went back at night, a night later. I went back to dig him up. But I couldn't find the spot! I'd left some shells and twigs crossed together on top. But the tide had come in and gone out and all the shells and twigs looked like crosses to me and I was digging on my hands and knees all night until Ed figured where I was and came and got me.

Enter Zivia in a traditional American Indian costume of brown suede shirt and pants. An eagle is embroidered on her chest with colored beads. She wears moccasins and a brightly colored feather headdress.

Zivia: Don't move, he's standing there next to you and even though he's cold and wet and you threw sand in his face, he says, "I forgive you, Mommy."

Ed: She's turned into a psycho.

Zivia: He says, "I forgive you, Daddy."

Pat: What is she saying—make her stop! Who told her? Did you tell her?

Cc: No.

Zivia: Isn't today Tuesday?

Ed: It's Sunday—what's wrong with you, Zivia? Are you on something?

Zivia: I'm a mystic.

Ed: You're not a mystic, Zivia. You don't even know what day of the week it is. Mystics talk in tongues, can you talk in tongues? You failed your Spanish Regents Examination or have you forgotten that?

Pat: She was going to be put in the advanced-placement track.

Zivia: I can hear all languages, all at once, all voices.

Cc: Zivia, what do the voices say?

Zivia: Hola, Bonjour, Ciao.

Ian: Zivia's trying her hand at practical jokes; very good, very stylish.

Zivia: Paul forgives you. He's happy now.

Cc: Paul? Paul Bennet the actor who—

Zivia: He lives now in the universe and the universe is love, love itself, unconditional love.

Ian: Okay, Zivia, we got it, enough.

Zivia: He says not to be afraid of hell, that there is no hell but expect to start all over from scratch.

Ian: Are we going to take pause now for the pubescent dementia of a—a—a makeshift Hiawatha?!

Zivia: God talks through me.

Pat: That's a blasphemy, Zivia. Is that any way for a Sunday School medallion winner to talk?

Zivia: Sunday School had everything wrong.

Ed: God, Zivia, your breath! What did you eat?

Zivia: Garlic. Garlic breath protects us from hearing lies.

Pat *(Recoiling)*: That's for sure.

Ian: You're a little Miss Know-it-all, aren't you, Zivia? If you were older or knew more you'd know it was smarter to keep your mouth shut three-quarters of the time and ask politely for things the other one-quarter. And you'd know also there is no God.

Zivia: Yes there is.

Ian: No, there isn't. There hasn't been one for years.

Zivia: Yes there is.

Ian *(His face defiantly up to hers)*: Prove it.

Without exertion, Zivia punches Ian in the face. Because her strength now is superhuman, this punch sends Ian flying back, crashing, screaming, and holding his bloodied face.

My nose. She broke my nose! My teeth.

Zivia *(Noncommittal)*: And if you say anything else I'll poke out your eyes and scalp you with my fingernails.

Ed: How did you do that? Anyway, that's no way to treat your uncle. Apologize.

Zivia: Blackie and Tang are here. They forgive you too.

Pat: Oh God, we forgot to feed the dogs!

Cc: Dogs go to heaven too?

Ian (*Holding his nose and mouth*): You think this is heaven?

Ed: Zivia, we're expecting some people who are going to listen to Daddy's play so can you just sit over there.

Zivia: We're doing my play.

Ed: Your play? What play?

Zivia: Form a straight line.

Ed: I've had just about enough of your shenanigans, young lady! You'll do as I tell you—

Zivia punches Ed in a quick succession, first fist in the chest, the second in the stomach. Ed doubles over in extreme pain.

Pat: Your father, Zivia!

Zivia: It's time to begin my play. Everyone get in a straight line.

Cc: Zivia, what's the play called?

Zivia: Stand up. You've got to stand up.

Pat: Get up, Ed. Zivia, Axel—Axel, he forgives me? He says that he's here and he's happy?

Zivia waves her hand, making "I Put a Spell on You" begin.

Cc: And there's a heaven, Zivia? There's a heaven? I've always prayed and known there was one!

Zivia: No heaven. Just space.

Screamin' Jay Hawkins: I put a spell on you.

Stand up and face this way.

Screamin' Jay Hawkins: Because you're mine.

In a line!

Screamin' Jay Hawkins: Stop the things you do . . . etc.

Do as I say!

Pat: Ed, get up.

Ian: My eye is swelling.

Zivia: Put your hands up over your head—straight up—and when I say turn, turn. Put them up!

Cc *(Hands up)*: No heaven?

Zivia: Eleanor Roosevelt says it's better to light one candle than to curse the darkness.

Pat: Is she here too?

Zivia: Yes. Now turn!

They all turn in time and from now on take all Zivia's stage directions.

Ed: What are we doing? The VIPs are going to get here—

Zivia: Turn! Turn again! Now rock! Rock right! Rock left! Hands up! Turn!

The doorbell rings.

Ed: They're here!

Cc: I should get that.

Cc goes to open the door. With a slight push Zivia sends her flying to the floor.

Zivia: Stay in line!

Pat *(Helping Cc up on her feet)*: I'm sorry we fought, Cc, I do like you, I just thought you frowned on me.

Cc: I didn't.

The doorbell rings again.

Zivia: Get in line. Turn!

They don't stop this dance, which is basically facing front in a line and rocking right to left with hands up in the air and turning on cue.

Ed: I'm sorry we didn't get along, Ian. It's just Mommy always liked you better.
Zivia: Turn!
Ian: But Daddy liked you better.

The doorbell rings, accompanied by knocking.

Ed: They're here, Ian, they've come, they're here!
Ian: Yes, but who?! None of those people Cc wrote to would come here—they were the ones who fired me—they hate me!

More knocks and doorbells, louder.

Zivia: Porter!

Porter opens the lid of the coffin he has been in and sits up. His face is expressionless.

Porter, pick me up! Carry me!

Porter gets up and out of the coffin. Zivia, from her standing position on the couch, stands up on Porter's shoulders. He grips her feet. Both standing, Zivia grows ecstatic. Lightning reveals from the window the murky shadows of the assembled figures outside. It looks like Judgment Day.

They're here, all souls, all souls in space singing backup! Virginia, Jody, Andrew, Peggy, Ruth, Sarah, Luisa, Floyd,

Howard, Anne, Timmy, Jamie, Dora, Felix, Luther, Edna, Hannah, Becca, Buddha, Jesus, Rama, Moses, Mohammed, open the door! Open the door! Open the door!

Cc, Ian, Pat and Ed turn around and, with hands up, face upstage. Loud thunder cracks. The knocking rattles the house. Lightning. End of song. Curtain.

THE END

Anteroom

cast iron painted white with two matching chairs. The floor is made up of black-and-white checkered tiles. Upstage there is a window; light from this window, according to the time of the day, is realistically rendered. Far stage left there is a door which leads into the kitchen and to the stairs to the help wing. Far stage right there is a door which leads into the dining room and to Mrs. Leland's living quarters. The effect of this seven-sided room with tall, gleaming cabinets with white-and-gold dishware is one of a cathedral. Although there is an old-fashionedness (1920s–1930s) about the decor, with the obvious contradictions of the sparkling appliances and the white, tip-top, freshly painted condition of the room, it should be impossible to tell what decade it is.

ACT ONE

SCENE ONE

Parker: Listen to me. Do you want to get ahead? Fasten your
apron.

Wilson: Won't it seem a little presumptuous meeting someone for
an interview already dressed in the uniform I would wear if
hired?

Parker: On the contrary, it will appear self-assured. Costumes are
very convincing, dress like something and you are that
something, period.

Wilson: I'm not equipped for the job.

Parker: Anyone can do it. I could even do it if I wanted to. You
have to want something to get it. *Change your attitude.* You
don't want to go home, do you?

Wilson: I can't go home.

Parker: Of course you can't! Tie the apron.

*The apron is tied. Wilson's uniform is complete: starched
white shirt buttoned to the neck, black trousers, long starched
white baker's apron and black loafers. Parker is wearing
extremely fashionable, up-to-the-minute, expensive summer
wear; it ill suits him.*

And whatever you do, don't mumble. You don't want to
appear an ambitionless blob all your life, do you? Say

your mother has a brain tumor, so you need this job to meet
medical bills. I used that story two years ago spring break
when I wanted to go to Palm Beach a week early. I just said
my father had a brain tumor—it sounds so invented no one
would imagine anyone could make it up.

Wilson: What do I do when she asks how much I want to be paid?

Parker: I told her you left your last job because the house wasn't
up to your standards—she loves that kind of talk—so she'll
probably ask what they were paying you there.

Wilson: But I wasn't working anywhere else—I've never had a job
like this.

Parker: *Make up a sum.* Never reason with a person from whom
you're trying to get money. Appeal instead to their fear of
being made to appear cheap. The trick is to do the least
possible work for the biggest possible rewards. And don't be
put off if she seems a little pilled-out.

Wilson: I read in a book how happiness comes from the pride of
hard work well done.

Parker: Forget that. Hard work gives you a bad outlook and as far
as pride's concerned, that comes from looking good. Fix your
cuff. Here she comes.

*Enter Fay, pale, thin, birdlike with short silver hair, wearing
a full-length, ice blue, sleeveless shift with white batik
markings on it. She has obviously taken more than several
tranquilizers. Her eyes are dilated; her voice, an aristocratic
drawl, imperious and far-off; her actions dreamy and slow.
Although she is not heavily made up, multiple facelifts make it
impossible to determine her age, which might be anywhere,
depending on her state of anxiety, from fifty to seventy.*

Fay: It's afternoon already.

Parker: Aunt Fay, this is that person Wilson I told you about who
can help you out of the fix you're in.

Fay: Fix? I'm not in a fix. Where is your father?

Parker *(Sending signals through the fog)*: Aunt Fay, we talked about this yesterday, remember? I knew somebody who could do the job because you need somebody since you lost the last cook.

Fay: I didn't lose the last cook. I let her go. She was a drug abuser and a nudist. And a bad cook.

Parker *(Wooing)*: True, and then I said I knew someone, very trained who's worked in London, England, right near Harrod's, your favorite store, in a little soup-and-salad restaurant and you said you loved soups, cold soups, remember? And then I said how he catered all these parties—very chic—in Manhattan, and then you, Aunt Fay, said you would throw parties again if you had someone like that. You remember now. Wilson, get Mrs. Leland a glass of water.

While Wilson gets the water, Parker continues in a phony sotto voce to Fay.

His mother has a massive brain tumor and probably needs a transplant. That's why he seems so withdrawn and shy, her illness is an economic burden, you'd be doing a good turn to hire him. I admit he's my best friend but that has nothing to do with it. *(To Wilson, same sotto voce)* Put it on a tray! *(To Fay)* You know, Aunt Fay, even though you're not really my aunt you're like a mother to me, closer because she's dead, so I wouldn't give you a bum steer.

Wilson serves Fay a glass of ice water on a silver tray.

Fay: Parker, find your father and tell him I need to speak with him.

Parker: What for?

Fay: Go now.

Parker: Well, is he hired or not?

Fay: The interview will begin when you leave.

Parker: Okay, but I hope you make the right decision. *(He exits)*

Fay *(Yet more imperious, more remote, underwater)*: First of all it

is of the utmost importance you realize I run a first-class
house. There are twenty-eight rooms and, when I was raising
my children, a full staff. There's only me now and I need very
little done. If you understand me, say Yes Mrs. Leland.

Wilson: Yes, Mrs. Leland.

Fay: In the hall near the stairwell there is a framed engraving of
my family tree. Next to it on a table there is a book of my
ancestry. I eat very light. Like most women I'm on a diet and
have to watch my weight. I enjoy simple but beautiful food.

Wilson: Yes, Mrs. Leland.

Fay: I can eat almost anything.

Wilson: I understand, Mrs. Leland.

Fay: Do you know how to use the microwave? Let me show you.
You put something in. Like so. And you turn it on. Like that.
Do you see?

Wilson: Yes, Mrs. Leland.

Fay: The ovens are in there. The other jobs are light and meager.
These include sweeping, dusting and vacuuming the porch as
well as, of course, all chambers leading to the dining area. My
car would have to be wiped dry with rags each morning
because of the dew. Have you ever done any simple serving?

Wilson: Simple serving?

Fay: Serve on the left, remove on the right. The Guatemalans were
here for ten years. I had the youngest serving beautifully by the
time she was nine. Then there was that earthquake and they said,
(Same voice although she believes this is mimicry) "Oh, Mrs.
Leland, buy us a plane ticket so we can go and help our relatives
sort out the wreckage and then we will return." I granted them
the airfare, and they flew away and never came back.

Wilson: How ungrateful.

Fay: Yes. Yes, I thought so. Have I spoken about my milk? There
are two refrigerators. One for the help. That would be, of
course, the cook and Maya. Maya is my seamstress and
chambermaid. The other refrigerator is for me. As you can see
it is kept all but empty except for my milk which must never

be mixed up with the regular milk. This is it, do you see the container, *Think Thin*. And in the freezer, here my ice cream is kept, *Think Low.*

Wilson: Yes, I see.

Fay: This is the glass I take my milk in, on this tray. Never this tray. This tray is for lunch. Or this one. This one for breakfast. Or lunch. Never this one. This is for tea. Or this one. Never this one.

Wilson: I see.

Fay: The silver must be polished daily because we're so close to the ocean. The fine spray and the salt, do you understand? Sensitive people are attracted to the sea while crude people prefer the mountains. Do you find that so?

Wilson: Yes, always.

Fay: Yes, I find it so. I think you would enjoy working here, because, like me, you love beautiful things.

Wilson: Yes, I do.

Fay: I'm sure you're overtrained. I'm alone in the house so my appetite is especially small. There's the porch but I can't ask Maya to do that. It's a man's job to clean a porch. I've had very bad luck in recent years with my cooks. I had to let a girl go who was a drug addict and a nudist.

Wilson: I never use drugs and rarely undress.

Fay: That's very good. Very very good. Say my name at the end of your thought.

Wilson: Mrs. Leland.

Fay: Yes. Good. Whatever you were paid at your previous domicile, you will be paid here. *(Into the intercom)* Maya.

Maya *(Offstage, her voice from the intercom)*: Yes, Mrs. Leland.

Fay *(To Wilson)*: With this intercom I can communicate with you from my room. One buzz for Maya, two for you. *(Into the intercom)* We have a new cook, report downstairs immediately. *(To Wilson)* She's very flaky but nice otherwise I would have gotten rid of her. She's a very mixed-up girl. I like light, thin, chic food.

Enter Maya. She is short, ample, with a soft girlish face and voice. Her hair, strawberry, is piled loosely in curls on her head. Her uniform is a small white belted maid's dress with a ruffled apron and a small white ruffle of a maid's cap. She has a Scandinavian accent, speaks English well but as a second language, slowly and carefully.

Maya: Yes, Mrs. Leland.

Fay: Maya, this is our new cook and butler. You're to help him acclimate himself. *(Vaguely pointing)* The kitchen proper through there and the dining room through there. Tell him how I like my fruit salad cut. *(Midsentence she turns her back to leave)* When you're finished in here don't forget to show him the lovely sitting room for the help. *(She exits)*

Maya: It's strange that I should be working here when I was raised with servants in a wealthy house. My father was a count. I have my own house on Long Island. *(She holds out a small color photo of her house)* Look.

Wilson: Maybe I should try and find out where everything is.

Maya: I became pregnant by my husband when I was thirteen. He was my history teacher and we had to get permission to marry from the king.

Wilson: Is this the dishwasher?

Maya: There's a second one in the kitchen but it's old and doesn't work. I answered an ad in the paper to serve as a companion but Mrs. Leland said she was too young to have a companion. I had once apprenticed myself at a couture house in Paris for a year, so she hired me as a seamstress but then made me the maid.

Wilson: What is this?

Maya: The ice crusher. I never thought the age difference between us mattered. Then this year I found out my husband had a girlfriend, an older woman. That's the plate warmer. When this older woman was a young girl in Poland she was taken and put in a death camp but because they didn't use enough gas she didn't die but awoke naked among the dead. She hid then in a Russian prisoner's bunk, attempted an escape and was recaptured. But then the war was over and she was set free, went to America and married.

Wilson: That's interesting. There's a grate on the ceiling, do you see it?

Maya: She lifts it up in the hall outside her room and sometimes listens. But you can tell because of the shadow the grillwork makes.

Wilson: She can't hear us talk through the intercom, can she?

Maya: No, you have to press down on it. Haunted by concentration-camp nightmares she attempted suicide many times, one time walking into the water fully clothed at the beach so my husband pulled her out. That's how they met.

Wilson: I'm sorry, who are you talking about?

Maya: My husband's girlfriend.

Wilson: And they live together now in your house?

Maya: I felt sorry for her. I thought the best thing would be to leave the two of them alone. It will end in its own time and then my husband will call me back. If she could have some bit of happiness I thought . . .

Wilson: I think I can trust you so I'll tell you, I don't really know that much about cleaning. The only cooking and serving I've ever done was sandwiches and beers for my mother and her friends.

Maya: I've been here for six months and I can't go. I've tried to go but she won't let me. She insulted me once in front of her guests. She called me a stupid girl and I packed up and left and she called me on the telephone later at night and begged me to come back and when I did she hung up my clothes and spoke kindly to me. On Mother's Day none of her grandchildren called and she smashed all their pictures against the wall and when I asked her if she wanted them back she told me to burn them in a pail outside in the garage.

Enter Craig. He wears a Dali moustache, Persian slippers with turned-up toes, a jacket of sherbet-colored, plaid, Thai silk with an opposing-color plaid cummerbund. He behaves like an elegant, dignified gentleman. His voice is soothing. No matter what eccentric outfit he wears throughout the play, his manner is in complete opposition to his costume: he acts like a bank president.

Craig: Hello, Maya, how are you this afternoon? William, hello, I'm Parker's father, I believe we met Graduation Day. It's great fun your lending us a hand this summer, bravo! I regret to report Parker's off sulking somewhere. I delivered what I suppose was very disagreeable news for him. I'm letting everything go and moving to Gstaad. I've always intended to retire to Switzerland. Have you been to Switzerland, William?

Maya: I have.

Craig: It's the most civilized country in the world! Maya, be so kind as to get Mrs. Leland for me, would you?

Maya exits.

I'm so glad Parker has such a nice friend! He talks so much of you—you'd think you were the only friend he's ever had! He's not a happy boy! Maybe we're just mismatched. That happens in nature. We just don't seem to be able to communicate, to, to converse, with, with civility. We have certain artistic interests in common, I believe. But you know my son is just not a person at ease.

Enter Fay.

Fay: Retire! What is this tomfoolery I hear? Craig, you're a young man! How could you even be thinking about retirement? It's ludicrous.

Hollow laugh. They kiss on the cheek during the laugh.

Craig: I woke up this morning, Fay, and there was a little bird on my pillow and that little bird said to me, Craig Perkin lay down your burdens and follow me to freedom land.

Fay: Nonsense!

Craig: It's true! I've decided to sell the house, both galleries, the apartment and everything in them, my collection as well. I'm going to pack one dark suit and expatriate to the Alps.

Fay: I don't believe you, Craig.

Craig: The suit in all probability won't be that dark but the rest is true, Fay. I've really had enough. The trends, the fads, the long lunches, openings, big deals, little deals, the even longer lunches, keeping up so as not to drop behind, the wearing trips back and forth, not to mention the clockwork blowups of the multifarious personalities! I'm tired, Fay! You know how long I've been at this game. I had my first gallery when I was nineteen. It was no more than the size of the room we're standing in. And I'm not so young anymore. I've got to face the fact I'm starting to age.

Fay: Nonsense, I won't hear of it.

Craig: We both are, Fay, we've got to face it, the plain and simple viciousness of it, of time passing. Nothing to be done about it, right, Will?

Fay: Utter nonsense! *(To Wilson, suddenly, disproportionately furious)* What are you doing, standing around like some dopey child?! Didn't I tell you to attend to the porch? Go then now while you can still work by the light of day!

Wilson exits.

I have to tell them where and how to move! The time I've wasted giving instructions to servants!

Craig: Take it easy, Fay, it's his first day, isn't it?

Fay: What? Yes, maybe I should sell my house, sell everything and just move, where did you say? Deauville. Yes, I'm very fond of Deauville, of the horses.

Craig: Fay, you love this old house, you could never leave it. There's too much of you in it and then if you did where would I stay when I come out?

Fay: I told you after the tragedy, get rid of everything, Craig, start from scratch. *I* did. I told the decorators, "Start from scratch." Oh, I kept some of his suits and ties and some photographs, I'm not made of steel.

Craig: Let's not talk about it.

Fay: Sell it all! It's a good idea, Craig. I mean it. We'll have a big auction.

Craig: Actually I was thinking more in terms of Sotheby's handling it.

Fay: Oh, for the collection, of course, but for the furniture and objects and Ethel's things we'll hold a charity auction.

Craig: I don't know about charity, I was thinking more in terms of saving the money for retirement and for Parker if he considers continuing his education.

Fay: Of course, but, Craig, you just say it's for charity. Then you can get high prices for everything and all you have to do is make a small contribution and keep the rest. I represent several charities.

Craig: It's sweet of you to take such an interest, Fay.

Fay: You'll move in here! In the interim your house will be in uproar. You know how much room I have.

Craig: I couldn't put you out that way.

Fay: You'll save money, Craig, not having to stay at the Inn. They've raised their rates. And I have a new cook.

Craig: It might ease the transition for Parker living here close to his friend while we review some possibilities for his future.

Fay: There's a bond between us, Craig! There's no point in ignoring that bond!

Craig: No one's ignoring anything, Fay, just calm down. You're going to get yourself into a state and then we're going to have to call the doctors. Now, you don't want them here, do you?

Fay: As if they would come because they were called! Last time I called—and it was an emergency—it was on a Saturday and a

teenaged girl straggled in on Tuesday. There's no pill invented
strong enough for me to take for this world, Craig!

Craig: Don't sell yourself short, Fay.

Fay: Maybe they're all in cahoots, all of them.

Wilson's expressionless face appears in the window, looking in.

Craig: Now who's talking nonsense?!

Fay: Maybe not! We're too good, you and I, Craig—that's our
problem! We're too good and the world kicks us in the teeth!

*The end of each scene and act is punctuated by a sharp
blackout.*

SCENE TWO

*A few days later. Sunnier light. Wilson is dressed as before.
Parker is in a completely different outfit, equally up-to-the-
minute trendy but not at all seeming to come from the same
wardrobe as his previous outfit. He has several shopping bags
around him from the Southampton branch of Saks Fifth
Avenue. He is leafing through a fashion magazine.*

Parker *(Looking through the magazine. Tonelessly)*: She's pretty.
He's good-looking. She's pretty. He's good-looking. She's pretty.

Wilson *(Cleaning a tray)*: Don't you think there has to be more to
someone than an exterior?

Parker: No, I do not. *(Pointing to a picture in the magazine)* Do
you like this sweater? Better in red or green?

Wilson: I never thought a job could be so easy. She really doesn't
eat anything but melon slices and berries.

Parker *(Yawning, vaguely self-satisfied)*: I told you.

Wilson: And all your father ever seems to eat are vitamins or steak
so rare it only takes a minute to cook.

Parker *(Attention still glued to the magazine, automatic)*: He's disgusting.

Wilson: And you're sure he's not going to find out we go out to eat on his charge card?

Parker: Positive. He's in a fog. He's so into his stupid auction. He's talked himself into believing it's for charity in the hope of securing a small fan for his room in hell. *(Takes out a red sweater)* Look what I bought. It's the sweater from the magazine. It came in red or green. Which do you think I should have gotten?

Wilson: The one you got.

Parker *(Taking out a green one, otherwise identical)*: I got both. I fit between a small and a medium so I got both, a small and a medium. *(Takes out two more sweaters, one red, one green. Carelessly ripping off the price tags. No pause)* You know what I found going through my stuff? A paper I wrote at school called *The Fall of the American Empire: Hallelujah*. I got an F. Now of course that information is household but I was so ahead of my time that no one could deal with it. The Egyptians didn't think they were going to fall and they fell. The Greeks fell.

Wilson: What do you think of those statues of black people holding electric candles in the halls?

Parker: They're brainy.

Wilson: Oh. I like my room.

Parker: Well, don't get too happy, you don't want to be a scullery maid all your life, do you? I mean I like living here too but it's not mine. That's what makes you happy, owning something, not just visiting it and certainly not waiting on it. Get with it! Don't be so passive. Plan a future. When I got you this job and you never thanked me—

Wilson: Thank you, Parker.

Parker: You're welcome. When I got you this job I hoped you were only thinking of the immediate moment and wouldn't get quite so into polishing the silver. Have you ever actually considered what happens to people who don't plan a future? Things go all right enough, for a period, but then one day, and not too long afterwards, they wake up and their future is gone! This farfetched idea that people have unlimited possibilities is simply untrue. Put down that knife and listen to me!

Wilson: I'm listening.

Parker: You'll be listening a lot closer when I'm famous—I'll be engrossing then!

Wilson: Famous for what?

Parker: Who cares! Don't be so small-minded. One day soon this house will belong to me.

Wilson: How?

Parker: I don't know yet but somehow. Having grown up in the converted garage of this place it's poetic justice I should end up in the driver's seat. And don't think I don't know the reason up to now I've been generally ignored. It's because I don't possess a great deal of beauty.

Wilson: You look all right.

Parker *(Hellbent)*: *I know I do not.* But I know also that when my face is ten times its natural size and on TV or newsstands and I'm laughing or crying I'll be so happy then—yes I will be! Cameras will love me as they have loved other faces in the past. Light falls on certain faces in miraculous ways and transforms everything. Newspapers will pick up things no one has ever detected in me, things I haven't even detected myself—they're that way—and the combination of the three, lights, camera and publicity, will transform me in body and spirit and I will be immortalized as I am sure is my destiny. It is simultaneously a great comfort and a great distraction to be so sure but I am.

Wilson: Don't you think that sort of thing could isolate you from everyone?

Parker: What if it did—so what?! I hate these liars who say they wish they could just be one of the gang! No one in this country has ever wanted to be one of the gang—they want to be head of the gang.

*Joy enters. She is black, a former fashion model. More chic
than beautiful, she has spent every dollar that has come her
way on clothing, shoes, jewelry, hair, grooming and makeup.
She wears many very thick ivory bracelets (see photo of Mary
Cunard by Man Ray), carries herself elegantly and speaks,
here, velvetly.)*

Joy: Hi. Parker, do you remember me? Joy. We met at the Biennale
in Venice last year. I've been trying to call the house all day. Is
your father around? I decided to get in the car and just drive
so here I am. Maybe Craig confused the day he was expecting
me or I'm here a day early, I don't know. I'm something of a
collector like your father, Parker, and I've stopped so often
along the way my car is rather stuffed! The leaves and the
sunshine have left me quite lightheaded! I feel as though I've
been drinking champagne.

Wilson: Hello.

Enter Maya, same uniform.

Parker: Maya, this is Joy.

Joy: Hello, Maya, pleased to meet you. Is Mr. Perkin here? You
know, I stopped in town to buy a few things and met so many
lovely people. It's funny, I've been to the Hamptons so many
times but I don't think I've been to this particular one, the
South. There are certainly a lot of grand old houses. Doesn't
the front doorbell work? Maya, you have a charming,
genuinely sweet face. You definitely have a presence. Have you
ever thought of acting?

Maya: In some ways I feel that in every minute in my life I've been
acting.

Joy *(Not comprehending)*: Really? How interesting. I was recently
in fashion. It was lucrative, modeling, but I needed something
more fulfilling. That's how I met Mr. Perkin.

Parker: Maya, get my father.

Joy: Oh, your father is here, good.

Maya exits.

Parker: The answer is no I don't remember you from the Biennale in Venice which, by the way, was a nightmare in which I met a million people a minute and twice as many ugly paintings. My father's decided to sell the house and I don't mind telling you I'm glad because it only has bad memories for me of my father forever entertaining lousy so-called artists, has-beens, never-will-be's, and assorted dismal hangers-on, all peddling their useless junk and bad company.

Joy: What a funny kitchen this is with no stove.

Enter Craig.

Craig: Joy, can you forgive me?

Joy: Craig, at last!

Craig (*During this they kiss on both cheeks*): I've been buried alive, lost track of the days and forgot—forgive, can you ever—what day to expect you.

Joy: You've been a big bad rabbit and I've been an Alice chasing you about. Finally I got this address from the gallery.

Parker: The Phony Baloney Gallery.

Craig: Well, thank goodness for that and thank double goodness for my old old friend Fay who's helping me with so many things.

Fay enters. She is wearing a long-sleeved pink minidress with small white polka dots, white collar and cuffs, and gold, brocaded, high-heeled shoes. She doesn't so much walk as float and only pauses briefly, not changing her course, before exiting through the kitchen to the garden.

Fay (*To Joy*): Hello. How are you. I'm so pleased to make your acquaintance. Hello.

Parker: Hi, Aunt Fay.

Wilson: Mrs. Leland, are you hungry? Would you like lunch?

Fay exits.

Craig: I hope she's not upset. But that's just it, Joy, I invited you out here for a month before I realized the upheaval I was about to bring upon myself. I'm moving to Gstaad.

Joy: You can't leave New York, Craig, you belong in New York.

Craig: I'm going to put you up at the Inn, Joy. It's very comfortable and it'll be my treat and we'll see each other every day and have a wonderful month, a real good time! It's just that I cannot infringe any further on Fay's hospitality.

Parker: More like she would never in a million years let you have your girlfriend stay here.

Craig: You will hold your tongue.

Parker: Hypocrite.

Craig *(To Joy)***:** You understand, I know. There really are no problems in the world when everything is taken step by step. I got a letter today, Parker, from Stella.

Parker *(With emphasis)***:** Throw it a-way.

Craig: Stella was Parker's governess who—

Parker: She's an abortionist.

Craig: You will hold your tongue!

Parker: She is or she was—she told me so herself, that during the war—

Craig: Don't speak of things you're not old enough to understand. *(To Joy and Wilson)* She's retired to an exceptionally pleasant village in the Pyrenees where she runs a lovely spa.

Parker: It's a filthy bathhouse for people so old they go there to wash up before climbing into their coffins.

Craig: She writes that she's adopted a little child.

Parker: As if the design of the world weren't monstrous enough they allow Satanists to adopt children.

Joy: I adore children.

Parker: I don't. If I had one I would smack it and smack it and smack it!

Craig: Parker, if you force me I'm going to have to call Payne Whitney. The letter goes on that she would love to have you there for a time while you decide what you'd like to do with your life.

Parker: Well, I'm not going to live with her. I'll die first. I hate her. And that's final.

Craig: You will hold your tongue!

Parker: Yes and you hold yours!

Craig: I think you and I, Joy, should take advantage of the luscious sunshine and take a walk along the water. Do you have proper shoes on? Look what I'm wearing, the slippers you gave me! I'm using them as shoes I love them so much.

Joy: They look wonderful, Craig, but I think I originally meant them as a decorative gift. I didn't think anyone could actually wear them.

Craig: They fit.

Craig and Joy exit arm in arm.

Parker *(Calls out after them)*: I already know what I want to do with my life—why don't you ask me! I'm going to be extremely big and you're going to be a shriveled nothing in the dust! *Good luck, Joy!*

Wilson: Do you think your father will marry her?

Parker: Absolutely not! This is my father's pattern, to dangle semiexotic women to make himself feel young and then replace them. He's only married my mother. She's no threat—loonies like that never get anywhere no matter how well they're dressed. Before Joy there was some singer named Kee-wee or Koo-koo or something. One day he should have them all out on the lawn for a picnic, the U.N. of gold diggers!

Wilson: Maya said that riches don't matter, that all we can hope for in this life is to earn the exquisite love of God.

Parker: Who said that? Maya, the maid?

Wilson: She's not really a maid.

Parker: I know, she's not really the maid and you're not really the cook and I'm not really the Pope.

Wilson: She's just waiting for her husband to call.

Parker: Everyone's waiting for someone or other to call. It's easy
to figure out why my father wants to go to Switzerland.
Because it's a hangout for fascists.

Wilson: Fascists? That's not true.

Parker: What are you talking about?—I've been there! You can't
litter, you can't cross in the middle and if you sneak on the
bus they arrest you!—It's hor-ri-ble!

Wilson: I hated living with my mother. She's very vulgar and I'm
very refined.

Parker: Live-with-Stella-while-you-figure-out-what-you-want-to-do-
with-your-life. I'm interested in that like I'm interested in
jumping off a *bridge!*

Wilson: Maybe he was just threatening you and doesn't really
mean it.

Parker: You don't know my father. He says things casually like
that and then he *does* them. And he has the nerve to call her
my governess—she was no governess. She was a glorified—and
not by me—*housekeeper* who needed and needs still I'm sure
unlimited electrolysis! I loathed her! She always had these
huge, awful dogs around her! They died, why couldn't she?!
And I'd have to learn French. I hate French. But what if he
did marry her? As you can see his David Niven appeal is on
the wane. What if he did finally break down and marry one of
these flappers? I'd be stuck with nothing, shipped off to the
Pyrenees in a box marked Stella.

Wilson: Maya said Mrs. Leland was adopted but she has that big
family tree painted in the hall and that book of ancestry.

Parker: So? It's just one of her eccentricities. It's charming if you
look at it in a certain light. Gives her something to think
about. What is this sudden cult of Maya? Don't take her too
seriously, she's at that age women want young boys around
them so they won't feel the Reaper coming to town.

Wilson: She's not that old, she's youngish.

Parker: Believe me, she has seen thirty-five *come* and *go*.

Fay enters with loosely held, crazily cut flowers from the garden.

Fay *(Vaguely)*: Who was that woman who was in here before?

Parker: Nobody, just some girl that's bothering Dad.

Fay: Oh. Yes. Of course, yes, I see.

Fay exits, some flowers fall on the way.

Wilson: Maybe she shouldn't take so many pills. She looks very unhappy.

Parker: I just thought of it! My father should marry Fay! It's obvious she has a big crush on him—God knows why. They'll have to go on a honeymoon—she has another house somewhere, I'm pretty sure—she does, I'm positive—they could go and stay there and I could live here! When they're gone you could live with me as my personal valet. Wouldn't you like living here?

Wilson: Yes.

Parker: You said you didn't want to live with your mother and your mother's boyfriend.

Wilson: I would like to live here, very much, I would.

Parker: Of course you would!

The intercom buzzer followed by the voice of Fay.

Fay *(Offstage, from the intercom)*: Wilson, I won't be taking lunch today.

Parker *(Into the intercom)*: Fay, it's Parker. I really think you should come down to lunch. Wilson's prepared something special for you and I have some exceptionally interesting news for you.

Fay *(Pause, from the intercom)*: What news?

Parker: Just come down and you'll see. *(He clicks off)* There.

Wilson: There, what? I haven't made anything special. I haven't made anything at all. I haven't even gone shopping. All there is are melons. I gave her that for breakfast.

Parker: Don't worry, I know Fay. Get an already sliced-up one and stick it in the blender. Quickly. Do it! Are those almonds? Mix them in. Gstaad! A ski resort. An old rickety old man wants to go live in a ski resort. That's comic! Now blend it.

They turn on the blender; it blends.

Wilson *(Shouting over the machine)*: What is this going to be?

Parker: Soup. Is there milk? Oh good. *(He pours in the "Think Thin" milk)* Now, while I pour in the milk, get a rose from the floor.

Wilson: What for?

Parker: Don't ask questions, just obey orders.

Wilson *(Unmoved)*: They look like she cut them with her teeth.

Parker: Pluck the smallest petals. *(He samples the concoction)* Not almondy enough. There must be some almond extract around here somewhere. Last year it was Chichén Itzá, Chichén Itzá, literally fixated on Chichén Itzá. Walked around in public with a poncho and a serape. Here it is! Blend again. *(Blends again)* Set that little table! She can eat in here.

Wilson: Which bowl?

Parker: The white with the small pink hearts. *(He pours the thick liquid into the bowl)* Sprinkle it with the rose petals. There. Follow my lead.

Enter Fay, dazed.

Fay, did you just have a beauty nap?

Fay: What?

Parker: Because you look so beautiful. Wilson, don't you think Mrs. Leland looks especially like a knockout today? Don't you love her gold high heels?

Fay *(Vain)*: The doctor has instructed me to wear them for my arches.

Wilson: I hope you're in the mood for soup.

Parker: Prepare yourself, Aunt Fay, for some alarming and true news. I think my father has fallen in love with you and wants to marry you. Can you believe it?

Fay: That's nonsense, Craig and I, we're the best of friends, we're . . .

Parker *(Singing crazily for a moment)*: "Friends turn into lovers." It's happened before. Listen to me, Aunt Fay, I had a dream last night, I did. I had a dream in which my mother spoke to me.

Fay: She was a very, very wicked woman.

Wilson: Wicked in what way?

Parker: In this dream—and you know dreams are the maps of destiny—in this dream she said to me, quite clearly: Fay and Craig should marry, they're right for each other, Craig is crazy for Fay, it's high time they hitch up and so on.

Fay: She would never say such a thing.

Parker *(Miffed)*: Well, she's changed then—I know what I heard. Now, try some of this soup and Wilson will tell you exactly what my father said ten minutes ago when he was standing here. Go on, Wilson, tell Mrs. Leland what he said about her, being nuts about her and all, go on.

Wilson *(Slowly)*: Well, what he said was that he'd grown very fond of you.

Parker: It was more than fondness—he was in a virtual froth—he was frothing over her—be more explicit.

Wilson: He said that he . . . he loved you.

Fay: He said that? He used that word—*love?*

Parker: I said he did before, you didn't believe me.

Wilson: And that you shouldn't be upset at all about the affair he's having with this younger woman.

Fay: Affair with this younger woman.

Parker: Oh, she's nobody, just a passerby.

Fay *(A slow hurricane)*: Is this dirt on the floor? It's soil, earth. It's appalling. *(To the sink to wash her hand)* And the sink. It's deplorable. Look at this soap dish. It's disgusting. Rust marks from the soap pad. It's ruined. I'll be forced to replace it.

Parker *(Trying to change the subject)*: Ooo, it's hot in here Fay. Why don't you build a pool?

Fay *(Flinging open the doors of both refrigerators. To Wilson)*: Look in the refrigerator. It has a stink. It smells! Take everything out of it. Both of them. I want both refrigerators scrubbed with baking soda and boiling water to get rid of their smell. Look at you! Your shirt is all *blouson!* Don't you hang up your clothes or are they all balled up in the corner of your room! *(Seeing the empty "Think Thin" carton)* You used my milk!

Wilson: It was for the soup.

Fay *(Nearly screamed)*: *I'm a prisoner in my own home!*

Wilson: Why do you say that?

Fay *(Flinging the contents of the bowl on the floor)*: If you can't get a hot meal on the table *what am I but a prisoner?!* *(Sinking to the floor, agonized, increasingly lost in despair)* How can I eat from a kitchen like this? I can't. I simply can't. Can I? I can't.

Parker *(He takes the bowl from her hands. More simple than compassionate)*: Aunt Fay, you're going to marry my father and that's going to be the end of all your problems.

Fay *(This voice comes from a place so far within her she doesn't hear it)*: But I'm old.

Parker *(Deaf)*: I can assure you, Fay, my father has woken up and seen the light—you're the gal for him, take my word for it. Wilson, get Mrs. Leland a glass of iced tea. How long can a grown man fritter his time away with dumb bunnies, right? You have everything going for you, Fay, charm, cultivation, you name it.

Wilson holds up a jar of instant iced tea. Parker waves and nods to him to make it quickly. Wilson stirs tap water briefly into the powder.

Fay *(Humbly)*: I know men like to think they can attract younger and younger women and never take women their own age seriously.

Parker: That's a fallacy. What we need to do is concentrate on

bringing the two of you together. It's true, isn't it, that you're
having some charity auction of all the junk Sotheby's isn't
handling, right?—well, you're in charge of the charity scene
around here, why don't you two throw a charity dinner party,
hmm?

Wilson shakes his head to indicate to Parker no dinner party.

Maybe that's too much work—too much bother. *(More a
question to Wilson than Fay)* A buffet?

Wilson indicates no.

No buffet. Hors d'oeuvres?

Wilson indicates that's all right.

Hors d'oeuvres. A cocktail party!

Fay: A dinner party might be good.

Parker: No, all that food, Fay, it's not good—not chic, it's just not
chic and it's not cheap either. We have to maximize our
profits. *(He gets the iced tea from Wilson and hands it to Fay)*
Now, drink this fresh, minty, delicious iced tea and while you
and Wilson discuss what hors d'oeuvres you're going to pass
out I'll go tell my father you and he have to put your heads
together for this project.

Fay *(The anger is gone)*: This doesn't taste like freshly made iced
tea. It tastes instant.

Parker: It just tastes that way because it's sugar-free, drink it. *(He
exits)*

Fay: You know Parker is very sensitive, the way I am. He has an
artist's temperament and lives sometimes in the world of
imagination. Do you think what he said is true, that his father,
Craig, Mr. Perkin, that he could, after so many years?

Wilson: If you don't mind my saying so, Mrs. Leland, I think you
should stop taking the pills you take. The more you take them,

the more you need them. The more you need them, the more
nervous you become. The more nervous you become, the more
unhappy you become and the less things go your way.

Fay: I shouldn't need to depend on anything.

Wilson: Let me hide them for you, that will help.

Fay: I wouldn't tell my doctor. It would prove to him how strong I
am, how people age at different rates.

Wilson: That's right; out of sight, out of mind.

Fay: You must tell me if this work gets to be too much for you. Try
some of this Rust Off on the soap dish. I just know I have to
have everything clean or I get sick.

Wilson *(He cleans up the spilled soup)***:** I'll spend an afternoon
going over everything in here.

Fay: I think the honeydew is going. I don't know if Maya eats
honeydew but maybe the two of you can finish it. In fact, take
everything that smells old, anything that reminds you of the
old cook—these pickles and salad dressing—put them in a
bag. Do you know what to do with all these soap rinds?—
they're terribly inconvenient. On television they advertised
this little wire cage and I mailed away for it. *(She is holding
it)* You insert all the soap rinds like so and then somehow melt
them down to one bar. Do you see?—in the shape of the cage.
*(No pause, she washes, wrings and hangs up to dry a paper
towel)* After you use a paper towel like this, rinse it out and
hang it up on the towel rack, like so, to dry. Paper towels are
reusable.

Wilson: You close your eyes while I hide the pills.

Fay: Here. They're closed. Tell me some of your ideas for the
cocktail party. What will you serve? No greens, I've had my
gall bladder removed.

*Wilson places the prescription container of capsules on a high
shelf in the cabinet.*

Wilson: How about melon balls?

Fay: That's a possibility.

Parker enters.

Parker: I had an incredibly brilliant idea in the driveway: why not a costume ball? A costume charity cocktail ball. It's a fantastic idea. Call Maya.

Fay: What did your father say?

Parker: Oh, he's thrilled down to his Supp-Hose, don't worry about that. I told him the whole thing was your brainstorm and he became *very* interested.

Fay *(Buzzes the intercom)*: Maya, come down immediately.

Parker: Now, what hors d'oeuvres did you decide on?

Wilson: I suggested melon balls.

Parker: No more melon. Name something else.

Wilson: Deviled eggs.

Parker: Just plain deviled eggs?

Fay: I don't know if that will do.

Parker: You mean with curry, *curried*, right? *(To Fay)* Don't worry, I've seen them in *W.* You've got to come up with a costume, Fay, a real knockout. Now, let's see. Scheherazade? Odette? Snow White? What appeals to you? How about a little gypsy girl?

Enter Maya.

Fay: Maya, you must prepare for a large charity function. That means you'll have to design a costume for me.

Parker: A very lavish one.

Fay: Yes. Of course you'll be helping Wilson with the serving.

Maya: Mrs. Leland, you'll have to get outside help. Even with Wilson, I can't handle more than four.

Fay: Four? They'll be a hundred and four!

Maya: Mrs. Leland, I've told you I have no experience as a maid.

Fay: Don't talk back! I'm not hiring outside help.

Parker: Maya, we're trying to maximize profits for charity. We're asking everyone to pitch in and carry their load. *(No pause, to Wilson)* What should I go as?

Maya: I must then announce, Mrs. Leland, that I cannot work here any longer. Today I give you my notice.

Fay: I won't have it! I don't need this kind of help. You'll do as you're told or I'll throw you out!

Maya: Good, I want to go.

Fay: Don't talk back! And take off that clown makeup!

Wilson: Maya, I was just telling Mrs. Leland how much more beautiful she looks. She's decided to cut out her pill-taking.

Parker *(Eating a pickle from the pickle jar)*: You've stopped your pills?

Fay *(Instant new artificial calm)*: The important thing is that we all stay very cool. Maya, sit down here and relax yourself. Leave all the ironing for tomorrow. *(No change in tone)* Dinner might be a baked potato or some applesauce. *(She exits)*

Maya *(Grimly, no energy)*: Sometimes I think this job is making me stronger, that it was meant to be, then I think that what happens to us is we get sick inside so that we won't ever be able to feel right again.

Parker: Oh, don't be a spoilsport, Maya. All you have to do is stick a few canapes on a doily and pass them around on a tray: big deal. The hard part is coming up with a getup to get her to look like Miss Helen of Troy. Frankly, I don't care if she goes as a hydra so long as I have a good costume. I know one person who won't have any trouble coming up with a costume: my father. Every day is Halloween for Daddy Dada. *(He exits)*

Wilson: Were Mrs. Leland's husband and Parker's mother lovers?

Maya: They committed suicide together in a pact. Maybe we could go out for supper one night together. Once I went to a bar and a young man, younger than you, asked me to dance. It's true I'm wearing more eye makeup today and some lipstick.

Wilson: I certainly wouldn't describe it as clown makeup.

Maya: You're like a cat, the way you sit there.

Wilson: Am I?

Maya *(Whisper)*: Step away. Over here. Do you see the light from the grate? She's listening.

Wilson *(Loud)*: Well, I think I'll go and sweep the porch. Bye. *(He walks noisily across the room and slams the door)* She has a lot of time on her hands, doesn't she?

Maya: On a trip around the world she grew envious of a woman who had purchased a straw handbag at a market and bribed the captain to turn the ship around, which he did, to go back to the island they had just left but the outdoor shop had run out of the bags and although the cruise continued and stopped many times at many different places she could see nothing but the bag she couldn't buy and thought about it daily and had a bad time.

Wilson: Do you know how to make that, applesauce?

Maya: Just put a potato in the oven on Bake.

Wilson: For how long?

Maya: One hour. We have a break now.

Wilson: I still have to polish the silver.

Maya: You're the only one she hasn't warned me to watch you don't take anything. She trusts you.

Wilson: This is her favorite plate, isn't it? I like it. *(He throws the plate up in the air and steps back to let it fall, crash and break on the hard floor)*

Fay *(Buzzer, then voice, offstage, from the intercom)*: Maya—what was that? Did something break?

Maya: Nothing, Mrs. Leland, an old dish fell out of the cupboard but it didn't break.

Blackout.

END OF ACT ONE

ACT TWO

SCENE ONE

*It is the night of the costume cocktail party. There is the
muffled sound of merrymaking and the occasional burst of
laughter. When the door to the dining room and living room
swings open, the noise, of course, is louder. There are trays of
glasses and hors d'oeuvres in various states of use around the
room. The party has been going on for several hours. At the
top of the act Wilson and Maya have been running in and out
bringing in dirty trays of glasses and empty trays of hors
d'oeuvres and taking out clean and full ones. Maya is wearing
a maid's uniform which is black with a small white apron and
a miniscule black-and-white cap. Wilson has added to his
uniform a small black bow tie and a white servant's jacket.
When both Maya and Wilson are off Parker enters in a burst,
obviously agitated. The concept of his costume is Josephine
Baker. He wears a brown-skinned leotard and tights with
blackface makeup, to look like the famous black entertainer,
nearly nude. His costume is composed entirely of pearls
cunningly draped all about to recreate (in some ways
authentically and in other ways hopelessly) Josephine Baker's
look. He has no irony about his costume, takes no notice of it,
makes no attempt to vamp or camp on its comic potential.
One supposes he has gotten all he wanted out of the costume
earlier in the evening, and now pays no attention to it.*

Similarly, Craig, who enters after his son, is unaware of his own ridiculous costume, a Spanish bullfighter with a black flat-topped sombrero with a ring of black pompons dangling from the wide brim, black pegged pants, short black jacket, pleated shirt and bright red cummerbund, black patent-leather boots and a short black shoulder cape.

Parker: Leave me alone!

Craig: I demand an explanation.

Parker: You're an idiot. I can't talk to an idiot.

Craig: If you refuse to produce an explanation, the least you should present, as a gentleman, is a direct apology to Joy.

Parker: You are so out of your mind!

Craig: You have been bottomlessly rude to her since her arrival and this costume one can only interpret as yet another and deliberate attempt to alienate her. The combination of your attitude and attire reveals what I can only fear is an emerging racist bent.

Parker: You probably don't even know what my costume is supposed to be—Josephine Baker, for your information—a person who has absolutely nothing to do with your nutty friend Joy, as if I gave her two seconds thought when I thought of it! What about the KKK couple, you didn't get mad at them.

Craig: That was done in fun.

Parker: Oh, fun! *(He drinks from the half-empty champagne glasses on the trays)*

Craig: Can't we be friends, Parker? Say that it's possible.

Parker: It is if you do what I want you to do.

Craig: Tell me what will make you happy.

Parker: Marry Fay. Marry her and leave me this house—go move to her other one—give me the profits from the sale of our old house and let Wilson and me live here in this one.

Craig *(Kindly)*: Is Wilson your boyfriend?

Parker: What?! Are you insane?

Craig: There's nothing wrong with that. As you must know, many of the people I've entertained in our home—

Parker: I am going to be hugely famous and that is something you obviously can't deal with.

Craig: I don't want to fight with you, Parker. You obviously have a great store of hostility pent up in your heart for me linked I'm sure with your mother's tragic death which in some way it's natural you should blame me for but I assure you— *(He puts his hand on Parker's shoulder)*

Parker: Don't touch me!

Craig: If you behave like this I'm afraid I'll be forced to contact Dr. Gold.

Parker: The second most insipid man in America?—call him! Call all doctors! All they ever did was make fun of you!

Craig: They know nothing about me.

Parker: Oh yes they do! I told them about your *jackets!*

Craig: Is there no way you will make an effort for us to get closer?

Parker: Yes, I told you, go away with Fay and we'll be closer.

Craig: I haven't the smallest inclination toward marrying Fay. The idea is, in a word, preposterous and you're speaking totally out of turn to suggest to me whom I might or might not marry.

Parker: I suppose this means you'll be running off to marry Joy. Well, let me tell you, she's only interested in your money.

Craig: I have no intention of marrying anyone. My objective in giving up my profession and moving to Europe was to prepare myself for the eventuality of my old age.

Parker: You can't prepare yourself for something that's already arrived!

Enter Joy dressed as a "prisoner," in old-fashioned black-and-white-striped prisoner pajamas with matching baggy shirt and calf-length trousers and cap. She also has a ball and chain.

Joy *(Lovely)*: I hope you two aren't arguing over me. I told you, Craig, I wasn't offended in the least by Parker's costume.

Parker: Save your breath. My father just said he had no intention whatsoever of marrying you so I suggest you back into the

crowd and try to hook some other old man, God knows there's
no shortage of them out there, and don't let the makeup,
disguises and funny hats deceive you, the hands of death are
on them already and you won't have to wait long!

Craig slaps Parker.

I hate you! I hate you! I hate you!

Enter Wilson with a tray.

Wilson: The lavender hearts are so popular. People who say
they're on diets and can't eat anything see them and take two.

Craig: William, you're doing a first-rate job. Several of the guests
have made note and inquired as to who's that well-mannered
and attractive young man.

Parker: His name is *Wilson* not *William.*

Craig: I apologize, Wilson, if I've called you by your wrong name.

Wilson: It doesn't make any difference really, I don't care.

Craig: Parker, I must tell you I'm strongly considering telephoning
Payne Whitney first thing in the morning and, as we both
know, it would not be your first visit. There, I've said so in
front of your friend and shamed you!

Parker: You think I haven't told him? Told everyone that for no
reason you stuck me against my will in the loony bin for three
months?

Craig: You were obsessed.

Parker: I was depressed because you were going to send me to
spend yet another summer with stinking Stella who I've told
you a trillion times I hate!

Craig: Parker was obsessed with someone we had coming to the
house to do some landscaping, someone transplanting small
trees for us.

Parker: I was not obsessed! He was my friend!

Craig: I've told Parker repeatedly there's nothing wrong with
human sexuality. I've assured him.

Parker: Shut up!

Joy: Craig, I really think—

Craig: I've told him many of my business associates—most of my business associates are of that persuasion, I can name them—

Joy: Craig, let's go back into the party.

Parker *(A threat)***:** Maybe I'll just go back into the party and sing the little song I prepared to go with my costume.

Craig: Son, I assure you there isn't anything left you could do to shock the guests.

Joy: Craig, why don't we—

Craig: Joy, excuse me for my bluntness but it's true that I have no matrimonial aspirations so if—

Joy: I know that, Craig, what do you take me for?

Craig: Well, I apologize, nevertheless I think you should consider packing and leaving tomorrow. I'm thinking of moving up the date of my own departure. The atmosphere of bickering here is as far from my taste as anything can be and wears on my nerves but extremely. *(He exits)*

Parker: Payne Whitney! Payne Whitney! If he says that one more time I'm going to stick him with a fork!

Joy: Let's be friends.

Parker: No, absolutely not, no, under no circumstances. Wilson, come with me swimming.

Wilson: Swimming, now?

Parker: Yes, if not now when? The whole world's here, we can pick any pool. Put down your tray—don't you realize you're serving pigs?

Wilson: I don't want to be fired.

Parker: Stay then, stay until the crackle of the fat! *(He exits)*

Joy: How do you size up this scene here?

Wilson: What do you mean?

Joy: I mean, what gives?

Wilson: I'm not following you.

Enter Maya.

Maya: More hearts on a tray.

Joy: Maya, I was just telling Wilson that I saw a great analogy
between the three of us. You work here scrambling back and
forth with tidbits using all human effort not to change your
expression. Years ago when I was very young, too young to
make very clear decisions about anything and grateful to make
a great deal of money quickly, I was a model. I followed
directions from everybody. Do you see how my cheeks are
sunken slightly? I had my wisdom and back teeth removed.

*Not for the first time, but here certainly, a burst of laughter,
coincidentally, overheard from the party.*

Then I would stick a wad of chewing gum between my lower
gum and lip to give my mouth a pout. To smile more easily I
would spread Vaseline over my front teeth. Every night before
I went to sleep I drank eighteen glasses of water to whiten my
eyes.

Wilson: Widen?

Joy: Whiten, make more white. And then, later, when they're done
with you, when the person or group of persons who once had
a use for you become through with you, that's when the end
begins.

Maya: Yes.

Joy: The agency has a book which has a record of how many calls
you've gotten each week for bookings and as the years pass by
and the number shrinks down to nothing, you are phased out.
Don't you see? I wasn't yet thirty and I was finished!

Wilson *(No irony, no cynicism)*: Thirty? Isn't the usual retirement
age twenty-three?

Joy: Why should it be?

Wilson: Why should anything be?

Joy: That's right! Why should anything be! Why shouldn't I have
anything I want to have! If that crazy old man can have a
gallery why not me? I have better taste than anyone I know.

And when everyone gets good and sick of what's hanging on the walls I can sell scarves, pins, shoes, hats, bracelets—I have enough stuff in my suitcase to open a gallery tonight! I don't need Craig!

Wilson *(Calm, noncombative)*: I may be speaking of something I know nothing about but it seems to me there are already plenty of what you're describing.

Joy: Don't you think I know what I'm up against here? You two looked too smart to believe that oh-what-a-lovely-town. Please! You need a hatchet to cut through the hypocrisy! I wasn't two seconds up the lane before people started underestimating me.

Maya: Someone said something to you?

Joy: They didn't have to! I just look at people and I know what they're thinking.

Maya: I don't really think that anyone—

Joy: I know what people are thinking.

Maya: But listen to me, I'm sure a beautiful woman like yourself with your beautiful dresses and your car that—

Joy: How does a rabbit know a fox is coming? How does the hunter know when to pull the trigger?

Wilson: What?

Enter Fay. She is a butterfly. The effect and intention of the costume is beauty and delicacy not humor. Much care has gone into the construction; perhaps the wings are slightly iridescent.

Fay *(Grand, gay, the party has made her high)*: Wilson, Maya, whatever are you doing in here so long? More champagne. Infinitely more champagne for everyone.

Maya: There aren't many bottles left.

Fay: Nonsense, don't talk back. Pour and serve.

Joy: Have I mentioned how stunned I am by the sheer, resplendent beauty of your costume? Actually I don't believe it's a costume at all but a transfiguration.

Fay: It is pretty.

Joy *(Excessively coy)*: The truth is I'm terribly jealous!
Fay: Yes.

Maya is now holding a tray full of glasses.

Maya, stop fussing with that tray. Just take the bottle out whole and refill those retaining their glasses. And remember to wrap the cloth around the bottle the way I instructed you.

Maya goes to put the tray down.

Oh you have it now, take it out as is. Use your head, Maya!

Maya picks up the tray again, more shaky.

Now you're spilling them, Maya, please be careful.
Maya: I can't take this, Mrs. Leland, I tell you, I cannot, I cannot.
Fay *(Suddenly the nurse)*: All right, Maya, get ahold of yourself, I'm helping you, I'm leading the way and holding the door for you. Just follow me. Wilson, follow us with the bottle.

Fay and Maya exit.

Joy *(Taking a glass of champagne. Dry)*: He'll never marry her. I know men. Yes, a woman may hear an alarm in the distance, call it a day and settle down with someone who's a sliver of her expectations. But a man? The ego is the last thing to go.
Wilson: I don't think anything good will come for you here.
Joy: Don't you? And who are you? What will come for you?

Exit Wilson with full tray of glasses. Joy begins drinking the small quantities of champagne left in the glasses on dirty trays. These trays have cocktail napkins with smudged lipstick on them and shallow glass ashtrays heaped with cigarette butts. She drinks from these glasses with increased thirst. Perspired, she turns on an electric fan stage left. Much laughter from the party. Enter Fay. She does not stand near the fan.

(*Slightly drunk*) Oh, I'm so glad you've come back! I've so much hoped to find a moment when the two of us could chat girl to girl.

Fay (*Civil*): I must request you refrain from distracting the help. They're so easily distracted but the difficulty of procuring help is common knowledge.

Joy (*Completely normal, no nuance*): I think you don't like me because you feel threatened that I'll take Craig away from you but I have no intention of marrying Craig, we're just friends. There really isn't any reason to feel threatened by me. What I'm really interested in is making a fresh start for myself. What with rushing to and fro we never got a chance to talk and I'm afraid you got the wrong idea. I think you could help me.

Fay: Are you trying to hustle me?

Joy: I could marry Craig at a moment's notice.

Fay: Are you trying to blackmail me? Leave my home at once or I will have you removed by the authorities.

Joy: I'm not afraid of you! Craig has no intention of marrying you—he said so. It's true you two look about the same age but not in his mind. He talks about you as "my old friend," and I don't think he means old times.

Fay lets out a pained sound as if she has gotten a sharp punch in the ribs. She doubles over, clutching herself. She is now near the electric fan and her wings tremble and flutter from the breeze.

What's wrong?! I'm sorry! I'm sorry! What's wrong?!

Fay (*Head turned away from the audience, still doubled over, contorted*): Leave me alone. Get out. Leave me alone. Get out.

Joy, carrying her ball and chain, exits, running through the door to the kitchen. In a moment we see her for a second through the window as she runs off. Much laughter from the party. Enter Wilson with tray.

Wilson: Some people are starting to go. Mrs. Leland, are you all right? Mrs. Leland? Can I help you?

Fay *(Head bent)*: Give me my pills.

Wilson: Is it Joy that upset you? She's just jealous. Yes, she is. Mr. Perkin was in here, just before, you didn't see him, he slipped in and out and he was telling her how much he loved you.

Fay *(She is looking up at him, sad-eyed, lost, wings trembling)*: I don't believe you. Tell me you are telling me the truth.

Wilson: Of course I am, Mrs. Leland. What reason would I have not to?

Blackout.

SCENE TWO

The next day. Maya is back in the white maid's uniform she wore previously. The telephone rings.

Maya: Hello. Yes. *(Short pause)* Mrs. Leland, the call is for me, it's for me. Mrs. Leland, please hang up. *(Short pause)* Hello. Go on.

Longer pause. Enter Wilson with several cardboard boxes with divisions intended for careful storing of the champagne glasses. He opens the dishwasher and loads the clean glasses. He is back in his previous uniform—i.e. minus the jacket and bow tie, plus the apron. Maya is motionless on the phone.

Yes, I'm still here. *(Rather casually and unexpectedly she hangs up)* That was my husband.

Wilson: I called my mother yesterday. She got married. She wants me to come live with them. I'd rather stay here.

Maya: Do you think we could live here indefinitely?

Wilson: She would have to give me a raise.

Maya: She might.

Wilson: I'd need a larger room.

Maya: My room is large.

Wilson: Her room is the largest.

Maya: Yes, yes, and one day—you know she's old and not healthy—one day she will die and I have heard how people have willed their homes to their servants. If you don't like me even a little you should say so.

Wilson: Of course I like you. A lot. I don't think we should bother washing all these glasses. Let's just put them directly in their boxes. They're going to the attic anyway and by the time they come down they'll just be dirty again.

Maya helps Wilson take the dirty champagne glasses from the silver trays and put them in the boxes. They spill excess champagne down the sink.

Maya: Last night, before you fell asleep, did you hear the moaning from her room? She's taking her shots again.

Wilson: What shots?

Maya: They artificially induce her period so she can look younger. Although she's a monster and suffering, I envy her, to have something to desire, even a straw bag, something even to be disappointed by. Do you understand what I'm saying?

Wilson: Of course.

Maya: You don't really understand anything do you? What if your mother should surprise you?

Wilson: She doesn't know where I am. I wouldn't tell her. I'll take these boxes up now. *(He exits with some boxes)*

Maya: Later I'll go up and take the tops off the boxes. The spiders and the mice will be able with their tiny tongues to lick the dried champagne from the glasses and believe then in heaven.

Enter Craig in paisley bathrobe over silk pajamas and sultan slippers. He sneaks up behind Maya and covers her eyes with his hands.

Craig: Guess who!

Startled, Maya drops a handful of silverware. It crashes to the floor. Because of the sound, the covering over the grate of the ceiling opens. Although neither Maya or Craig notice, it makes a clear pattern of light on the floor, including, perhaps, the shadow of Fay's head moving close to the grillwork to listen.

Maya: You frightened me! Don't do that to me ever again, Mr. Perkin.

Craig: Oh shush, I only meant it as fun. Here, let me help you clean it up. *(He is on his knees)* You know I've had my eye on you since you arrived here.

Maya: You should have your eye on Mrs. Leland.

Craig: I'd much rather have it on someone as pretty as yourself.

Maya: Are you looking up my skirt?!

Craig *(Grabbing her around the knees)*: Oh you sexy little muffin, stay put while I bite your knees.

Maya: Unhand me!

Craig *(Losing patience instantly)*: Oh—unhand me!—what do you see yourself as, pray tell! Paying so much attention to a boy half your age. You're not seventeen anymore, my dear, I can assure you! I told my wife having children makes you weary and old before your time, makes you feel guilty for no reason, but she wanted one and I loved her so I complied and then she ran off with someone else—do you see how things work out, how things twist around to undermine and ridicule you?

Enter Wilson with more boxes. The shadow from the grillwork is gone.

217

Good morning Wilson—you see, I've remembered your name
correctly. I'm not yet quite so senile as Parker would have it.
You haven't seen him, have you? His bed isn't slept in.

Wilson: No, I haven't.

Craig: Well, no reason to worry. He's sulking somewhere certainly
as is his wont. Although I said I would not be requiring lunch
I've decided to take some toast points on the porch.

Wilson: Toast points?

Craig: Let Maya attend to it. *(Superciliously)* Would you Maya? I
need to talk for a moment with Wilson.

Maya takes bread out of the refrigerator.

Wilson: What would you like to talk about?

Craig: Maya, isn't it possible to make that in the other room?
Surely the kitchen can be used occasionally to prepare food.
You can slice it in there and toast it on one of the stoves. And
I'd like some mineral water as well. With lime.

Maya exits with bread.

I want your help, Wilson. It's become I'm sure to you painfully
evident that Parker is an exceedingly troubled young person
who at this juncture in his life clearly is capable of incurring
harm upon himself. As a response to this tragedy, because
that's how I think of it—when a child who has *every*
advantage, *every* privilege, *willfully* seeks to undermine the
harmony of all those who surround him and with belligerent
glee courts at every venue discord, then nomenclature fails me
and I am at a loss but to call it tragedy!

The intercom buzzes twice.

Fay *(Offstage, from the intercom)*: Wilson, I've decided to go for a
swim. As a result of this decision I'll be taking a light late

lunch. A scrambled egg in the double boiler, one pat of butter, low flame. Are you there?

Wilson: Yes, Mrs. Leland. One egg or two?

Fay (*Offstage, from the intercom*): One.

Craig: As a response to this situation, I've made certain arrangements for Parker to be set for a period of time, contingent upon his adjustment, in a place where people possessed of godly patience prompted by financial gain will be better equipped to deal with the particular tribulations of my son. Firstly, I need to know where he is.

Wilson: He's not here.

Craig: I know that. When he is here, for he will inevitably come here to see you, I may need your help. I'm depending on you to recognize this is all for the best.

Craig exits. Enter Maya with toast points on a plate and mineral water.

Wilson (*Pointing*): He went that way.

Parker's face pops up in the window. Wilson sees him but, although the face is startling, Wilson is not startled. Maya puts the plate and glass on a tray and exits. Enter Parker. He is still in his costume, which is now in a state of complete disarray, strips of pearls dangling disjointed, one stocking drooped around his ankle, and all makeup very smudged. He carries a small package.

Parker: Hi. It's me.

Wilson: Hi, where've you been?

Parker: At the beach, swimming, walking around, thinking.

Wilson: Like that?

Parker: Of course, what of it?

Wilson: Did anyone see you?

Parker: Truly I am beyond caring what sunbathers think of me. Guess where I went last night. Joy's room at the Inn! She's going to help me kill my father. She's turned out to be a good egg after all.

Wilson: You're going to kill your father?

Parker: Yes, why not? I'm sure it wouldn't be the first time anyone's thought of it. Maybe it's even a good idea.

Wilson: Why are you going to kill him?

Parker: Clearly to get him out of the way. Are you thinking of the Ten Commandments? Well, let me tell you, I *hate* the Ten Commandments! Constructed entirely by a patriarchal society for the sole purpose of keeping the people checked and in place! Deliver me from the Ten Commandments, amen.

Wilson: How do you plan to do it?

Parker: Scare him to death. Few people know he has a heart condition but he does and he takes more pills for his problem than even Fay. All he needs now in my estimation is a good jolt in the form of a pantomime staging the double suicide of my mother and Fay's husband Henry. I'm going to play my mother and Joy's going to play Henry. She likes to act and it'll probably be her only chance to play a dead white man. She told me an interesting idea she has for an all-black version of *Othello*.

Wilson: You said she was crazy.

Parker: Crazy is just a way of addressing your life head-on.

Wilson: And she agreed to do it?

Parker: Not at first, but in return—because my father will be dead or in a coma or in a home for the semidead—I promised her one of these two houses.

Wilson: Did she believe you?

Parker: I was telling her the truth. After all, we won't be needing both of them, right? She can turn it into a chicken coop for all I care.

Wilson: Could you live with yourself knowing you'd been responsible for somebody else's death?

Parker: I most certainly could! Couldn't you? Think about it. Lots of people live with that idea, hundreds of people—she did— my father did.

Wilson: Do you blame your father for your mother's suicide?

Parker: Absolutely not! If someone wants to kill him- or herself, my advice to that person is get right to it, don't dawdle.

Wilson: What about her, Mrs. Leland, will she be at the show?

Parker: Yes, if we're going to the trouble of putting her dead husband in it she might as well be there.

Wilson: Will she be scared to death too?

Parker: Maybe, who knows, the change would do her good.

Wilson: Maybe you should try being nicer to your father, it wouldn't cost anything.

Parker: Cost anything? My life! Mark my words, that man will be my executioner! Who was it who said we must despise our immediate predecessors—he was talking about my father!

Wilson: And you think this thing with Joy and you is going to work? It wouldn't be believable.

Parker: Are you kidding?—anything's believable. Once you decide to break with the thin veneer of civilization—which, by the way, so few profit from—what isn't possible? The whole world is on a lift-yourself-by-your-bootstraps project but what good is it if it only gets you to the curb? At school remember they kept trying to expel me—they were threatened by my mind, that it wouldn't fit their one cookie-cutter shape! Stop playing with everything and listen to me!

Wilson: I have to clean the refrigerators. I promised Mrs. Leland I would.

Wilson empties one of the two refrigerators and stacks the metal grill shelves to the side out of the way. He puts on rubber gloves and sponges the inside of the white refrigerator.

Parker: Oh let us be industrious every split second of the livelong day or the other industrious little ants will nudge us out of our place in the ant hole!

Wilson: Don't you think you'd feel better, Parker, if you just took every day day by day?

Parker: No, I don't! That's the advice people give to people who they don't want to get ahead. That's the advice I told you they gave me at the hospital and I would never have told you that if I wasn't so sure there was nothing wrong with me. But the day will come—and how I'll laugh!—when I see my oppressors fall and fall and fall! We must fix our faces to appear bad because goodness is mistaken for weakness and it is despised!

Enter Maya.

Maya: Your father's having bread and water out front.

Parker: Good, a fitting final supper! Maya!

Maya: Yes?

Parker: Guess what my father thinks—that Wilson and I are boyfriends. Isn't that nutty?

Wilson: Yes.

Parker: Why do you say yes so automatically?

Wilson: Because, it's as you say—nutty.

Parker: I bet you two are having sex—are you?

Maya: It's a bagatelle.

Parker: Is that so? In other words I don't exist.

Wilson: You're my best friend.

Parker *(To Maya)*: Your husband is not coming back to you— that's over! Wilson told me. You don't think we talk? We're best friends! You're living in a fantasy world, my dear little maid. I don't mean to be cruel but people who look at things unrealistically—it really gets me!

Maya: I've stopped waiting for him.

Parker: She looks ready to shove off on some barefoot pilgrimage, passing out loaves among the multitudes—are you ready for that? To give yourself up to other people you have to give up your possessions. If you give up your possessions you give up your power and if you give up your power you evaporate!

Maya: Some people want to evaporate.

Parker: Let them.

Maya exits.

I better hurry and get into my costume. *(He unwraps his little package, which contains a crumpled navy blue dress with cut crystal buttons and a small hat with a veil. He puts this on over his other costume while continuing to speak)* I had the stroke-of-genius idea to fill a Baggie with vegetable cocktail and tie it with dental floss. We just have to stick it in the grillwork up there, let it dangle down and at the appropriate cue, pull on the floss and down comes the blood, freaking Daddy out.

Wilson: I thought you said they did it with pills.

Parker: Blood's scarier. Where's Fay?

Wilson: She said she was going swimming.

Parker: Swimming? We better hurry. Hold the chair while I stick this up there. How do I look?

Wilson: Not good.

Parker climbs on top of the chair and places the red filled plastic pouch into the ceiling space behind the grillwork, letting the dental floss dangle down. Wilson holds the chair. While performing this task Parker talks.

Parker: You think I look bad, wait until you see Fay's I'm-going-swimming get-up. She puts on this faded blue cabana suit, you know with hot pants from when dinosaurs ruled the earth. Then she spreads Vaseline over her whole body to protect her surgery scars from the sun. She's had every liftable thing lifted. Then, and I'm not making this up, she wraps herself in plastic dry-cleaning bags so she won't get the Vaseline on the furniture. She looks like a pupa. There, how does that look?

Wilson: It's noticeable.

Parker: Not if you dim the lights and squint, it disappears.

Enter Joy.

Joy!—you have to get in costume. Did you bring your makeup?

Joy: We need to talk. I've been thinking and I'm not comfortable with this whole idea. It's too crazy.

Parker: It's foolproof! You can't back out now! Tell her Wilson. Just slip this suit over what you're wearing and you'll be fine. *(He dresses her swiftly with a dark suit from the package his dress came from)* We have to band together, Joy, all of us! Remember what you said at the Inn, how oppression reigns because of cat and dog factions? *(Looping an already knotted tie over her head)* Wilson, help with this tie.

The intercom buzzes twice.

Fay *(Offstage, from intercom)*: Where is my scrambled egg?

Parker: Stall her!

Wilson *(Into the intercom)*: It's on its way, Mrs. Leland. I'm using a low flame.

Parker: You haven't started her egg yet—good—that way she'll come down looking for it and find us! Dim the lights.

Joy: I'm telling you I don't want to go through with this.

Parker: You have to do it! Or I'll tell everyone it was your idea! Somebody's coming! Just say in a spooky voice they drove you to it—fill in the blanks and make it up as you go along. Everyone get into place—hide!

Throwing brooms and mops out quickly, Parker hides in a broom closet and shuts the door. Joy, for a moment at a loss which way to run, gets into the already open and shelfless refrigerator and shuts the door.

(Opening and shutting the door of the broom closet the instant before his father's entrance) Dim the lights!

Enter Craig in a darker, more conservative suit than his usual outfits. He looks worried and older.

Craig: That fickle little servant girl threw my lunch at me!

Wilson turns off the lights but because it is late-afternoon summer, much light still enters from the window.

Why are you turning off the lights?
Wilson: To save electricity.
Craig: Fay's got you on her skinflint regime too. She had the nerve to hand me a bill with my phone calls itemized on it! Is he here? I had them bring the van around to the back so we only have to get him through the kitchen.

The broom-closet door opens and Parker steps lightly out of it with outstretched hands. In a further attempt to appear ghostlike he speaks in a wavery voice, haphazardly falsetto.

Parker *(Ghost voice)*: I am your dead wife. You are responsible for my untimely death. I've come to chariot you off to hell.
Craig *(Nicely)*: Parker.
Parker *(Ghost voice)*: Don't walk any closer to me. I breathe air from another world and don't call me Parker, I'm my mother Ethel—I mean I am Ethel your wife—
Craig: Parker, what are you doing?
Parker *(Sotto voce)*: Psst—Joy, this is your cue—where are you? Wilson, pull the string.
Craig: Parker, come with me outside, would you, so we can talk together outside?
Parker *(Ghost voice)*: I bid you to croak. *(Sotto voce, to Wilson)* Pull the string now—what's wrong with you?! *(Suddenly he feels a bug on himself and jumps frightened, swatting his neck and shoulder)* There's a bug on me get it off! Get it off! Oh, it was only the veil, oh well. *(To Wilson, ignoring his father now that the pantomime has been such a flop)* Where did she go? Why didn't you pull the floss?
Craig: Parker, let's go out together, you must be terribly warm with all those things on.

Parker *(To Wilson)*: You deliberately didn't help me! It was my
idea to put red cabbage and sour cream together for the
lavender hearts and you took all the credit. *(To Craig)* I
fooled you—he's not really a cook!

Craig: Let's go now, okay?

Parker: What's outside that you want me to go there so badly? No!
I don't want to go back there, no!

Craig: Come on, Parker, I warned you.

Parker *(Panicked pleading, trying to make light of it)*: Daddy!
I'm sorry! Whatever you didn't like that I did I won't do. I'll
go visit Stella! You wanted me to visit her and I will.

Craig: Of course, of course.

Parker *(Superior)*: What do you mean, "Of course, of course"—
don't talk to me as if I were insane, "Of course, of course"—I
only wish I were insane, it would be a consolation! Now, out of
my way.

*Parker exits through the kitchen. Once through that door, we
hear, he is grabbed by orderlies. He screams, kicks, puts up a
fight. Craig exits after a moment to help. The door blocks the
combat from view although it is kicked frantically by Parker.
Wilson remains alone staring in the direction of the battle.*

(Shouting from offstage) Let go of me! Let go of me!
Assassins! Assassins!

*We hear the sounds of Parker's feet being dragged out, the
mumbling and struggling of the orderlies. Parker is still
yelling as we hear the doors of the van bang shut and the van
driving away over the gravel. Craig enters. He is disheveled
from the struggle.*

Craig: Wilson, I'd like to avoid Mrs. Leland if at all possible. I'll
write her a note when I get to Gstaad. I'm leaving for
Switzerland in the morning. I'm following the van to the

hospital now to sign the necessary papers and directly from there I'll spend the night in New York. This has all been too much for me. I must take one of my pills.

Craig opens the refrigerator. Joy is perched within. Shocked, Craig lets out a sound of alarm.

Joy: Hello, Craig. It's Joy.
Craig: Joy! What in the name of—
Joy *(Stepping out of the refrigerator)*: I was just—
Craig: *I don't want an explanation!* I had a feeling you were psychopathic.
Joy: Craig—
Craig: I'm leaving the room and if and when I return to this room or any other room in this house or any other house anywhere at any time I expect to find you gone. I have articulated my feelings. Goodbye.

Fay enters as Craig exits, using the same door stage left.

Hello Fay.

Running, Joy exits right. Fay is wearing what Parker described: a faded old blue bathing suit, Vaseline, plastic dry-cleaning bags.

Fay *(Vague)*: A big rush. Well, let him go, let everything go, hello and goodbye. *(Fake laugh)* Somehow it is so easy, so seductive, to get drunk on *hope*. And then of course everything is on this . . . this *trajectory*, a giant trajectory hurling us toward . . . I don't know what.
Wilson: I'm sorry I'm late with your egg. I'll go to the kitchen and start it right away.
Fay: I no longer want the egg, I want my capsules.
Wilson: But, Mrs. Leland, don't you think that—

Fay: I don't want to think, I want my pills. I'm giving you notice your services will be needed no longer.

Wilson: Mrs. Leland, the egg burned because I was busy cleaning out the refrigerator, do you see? I'll take a reduced salary—I'll work for free. Remember you said that you could tell we both loved beautiful things? I do. At night, I come downstairs and sit in the living room with one lamp on and I pretend this is my house. I don't want to leave.

Fay: I said you're fired.

Wilson: Well then maybe I could just live here as your guest.

Fay: Give me my pills, pack your things, and prepare to depart at your earliest convenience.

Wilson: Mrs. Leland, Maya said you had put an ad in the paper for a companion and even though you're too young to have one maybe I could be that. You don't like outside help and it's too much for Maya alone. Maya might even leave—I could do her work. You need someone to take care of you and I could do that—I want to.

Fay: Your deportment is unacceptable and your employment terminated.

Wilson (*A mock search for the pills*): I can't seem to remember where I put those pills. When I find them I should take a couple myself, Mrs. Leland, because I've been pretty nervous. The last time I slept someone spoke to me in my sleep. The voice said your real parents, Mrs. Leland, were ne'er-do-wells who couldn't afford to keep you and that anyone thinking of marrying you should check their family tree because they'd be marrying beneath their station.

Fay: Get out of my house!

Wilson: No, they're not in here. I don't believe in ghosts but last night I heard moaning in the hall. For a minute I thought it was you, Mrs. Leland, but when I got closer I realized it was a younger woman and she wasn't alone, she was with a man and I heard them say that *because you were making them so miserable they decided to kill each other* and I was so frightened I called out no!

Fay: No—

Wilson: Yes—here are the pills—I found them! Which glass should
I use? This one or this one? How about some *Think Thin* to
wash them all down? *(The pills fall on the floor)* I was so
frightened, Mrs. Leland, that I held my robe up over my eyes
because I didn't want to look. Like this. *(He brings up the
bottom of the apron as if to cover his face and pulls the string
attached to the grill. The red juice pours onto his apron and
he yells, seemingly truly frightened)* Do you see? Look! Look,
Mrs. Leland! They're up there now—look!

*Fay screams and faints. Just as she faints Maya enters and
catches her by the shoulders while Wilson catches her by the
legs, so that she never falls to the floor. Wilson is instantly
transformed to concern.*

Maya—catch her! She spilled her tomato juice. It must have
reminded her of something.

Maya: We should put her up on her bed and call the doctor.

*Maya and Wilson exit carrying out Fay. Joy has been watching
the last bit of this from the kitchen door. Joy enters. She still
has the suit and tie on over her dress. She collects the spilled
pills in her fist. A woman, Barbara, taps on the glass window.*

Barbara *(From the window)*: Anybody home?

Joy: Who are you?

Barbara: I'm Barbara, can I come in?

Joy: I don't know.

*After a moment Barbara enters. She is at least forty and
rough. She has dyed hair and coarse, contemporary casual
clothing.*

Barbara: Holy Moly. Look at all this silver! You're not Maya, are
you? I got a call from a girl named Maya, am I saying that right?

229

Joy: She's upstairs.

Barbara: She told me I should come for my son Will which is what
I wanted to do anyway but you know kids when you get
remarried, what are you wearing? Anyway, so I drove with my
boyfriend—actually my husband! As of recently. I mean, you
know, you wait all your life for something good to happen and
then it *does!* What a kick! I am crazy for this guy—he's
younger than I am—I know that doesn't matter at all
nowadays and I look much younger than I am but I thought
let them see you have a child half grown and they'll think
you've got to be a Methuselah or something I'm telling you so
who could blame me keeping Will a secret but when I told Tom
he was flabbergasted I had a son—thrilled—go figure it, you
can't predict things.

A car horn honks.

He's going to be a good disciplinarian too, Tom.

Enter Maya.

Hi, you're Maya, right? I'm Barbara. *(To Joy)* What's your
name?

Joy *(Barely audible)*: Joy.

Barbara: Happy to meet you. Who wants a cigarette?

The car horn again.

That's Tom, not too patient! I should get your numbers, Labor
Day we're going to have a big barbecue. What is this room
anyway? I thought I passed through the kitchen on the way in.
Doesn't matter. Just between us I'll tell you something. It
wasn't easy for me. Okay? I had a young son to raise and a
husband who liked the booze and did a disappearing act—no
one wanted to know me from *Adam.* Why am I saying this?
Because I have been down *twice* in my life and no one came to

help me. Not family, not friends, certainly not family! I have a
word to the wise—it's not too good to be too good in this world
because they *fuck* you, excuse my French but they *fuck* you
and then they *fuck* you again! I used to be a chain smoker. I
gave it up for two years then I thought *what the fuck for?*
(She lights a cigarette quickly and takes a long drag on it)
Roll with the punches they say. You know what I say? Fuck
'em. Why should I have them over for dinner? Now if I have
them over at all I have them for drinks. No more lamb chops
and no more candy! You're nice ladies so take my advice, it
doesn't pay to be nice. I used to be nice. *Take my advice:*
THINK ABOUT YOU. Let me shake your hands.

Enter Wilson. He has removed his apron.

Wilson: What are you doing here?
Barbara: What-am-I-doing-here is right telling people I have a
brain tumor. I'll give you a brain tumor you'll never forget—
with the back of my hand!

The car horn honks.

That's Tom, get in the car.
Wilson: Maya, tell her I'm going with you. Maya.
Barbara: Move it!

The car horn honks repeatedly. She takes a silver tray.

I'm taking this tray for his pay—see—I'm not stealing. *(To
Wilson)* It'll be your wedding present to me and Tom. Now, get
in the car. Get! Now!

*She pushes him out the door by the collar. Eventually the car
horn stops, the car doors bang open and shut and we hear
the car pull out recklessly over the gravel.*

Maya: I read a short story once where a woman goes to the ladies room and while she's fixing her makeup in the mirror she doesn't know which woman in the reflection is herself and which are the others. She begins to wish to be one more than the others but soon one by one they all leave and the one she least wanted to be is the one she is. So she takes a clip out of her hair which lets it hang down and removes an initial pin from her lapel and, taking off her shoes and stockings, she leaves the building feeling hot beach sand under her feet even though she's really in New York City.

Joy: When I was a model my booking agent wanted me to remove my bottom ribs to give myself a sleeker waist. Sometimes I think everything would have worked out better for me if I had.

Maya: Maybe sometimes it's not so hard to break with everything, to drop even your initials.

One buzz from the intercom.

Joy: She didn't die?
Maya: Who? Oh, no. Can you cook?
Joy: What?
Maya: Can you cook at all?
Joy: Of course, but—
Maya: And you wouldn't mind cleaning?
Joy: Here?
Maya: You could if you wanted to. She would hire you.

One buzz from the intercom.

Fay *(Offstage, from intercom)*: Maya, are you there?
Maya: My husband called before and I hung up on him. I thought I'd been waiting for him to call but I wasn't waiting for him at all. I don't know exactly what it is I'm waiting for but I want to be ready. I know that when you're ready you turn your back and then it comes and taps you on the shoulder.

Fay *(Offstage, from intercom. They ignore it)*: Maya, are you
  there?
Joy: I don't know what to do.
Maya: Loosen your tie.

The two women are sitting on the two chairs. Blackout.

THE END